# The Kids' Book of Divorce

# The Kids' Book

## By, For and About Kids

# of Divorce

By: The Unit at Fayerweather
Street School

*Edited by Eric E. Rofes*

Vintage Books
A Division of Random House
New York

First Vintage Books Edition, September 1982
Text and illustrations copyright © 1981 by
The Lewis Publishing Company, Inc.
All rights reserved under International and Pan-American
Copyright Conventions.
Published in the United States by Random House, Inc., New York, and
simultaneously in Canada by Random House of Canada Limited, Toronto.
Originally published by The Lewis Publishing Company, Inc. in 1981

Photos appearing on pages 5, 11, 14, 15, 22, 25, 28, 33, 34, 72, 76, 85, 91, and
113 were taken by Laura M. Spiro.

Library of Congress Cataloging in Publication Data
Fayerweather, Street School. Unit.
The kids' book of divorce.
Originally published: Lexington, Mass. : Lewis Pub. Co., 1981
Bibliography: p.
Includes index.
Summary: Twenty school children, fourteen of whose parents are divorced,
discuss the various aspects of divorce and give advice on coping with the
feelings, fears, and problems caused by divorce and its aftermath.
1. Divorce—Massachusetts—Cambridge—Juvenile literature.
2. Children of divorced parents—Massachusetts—Cambridge—Juvenile literature.
[1. Divorce]
I. Rofes, Eric. II Title
HQ836.C2F39 1982    306.8'9    82-4921
ISBN 0-394-71018-5    AACR2

Manufactured in the United States of America

**98765**

# Contents

*To the past, present and future children of divorce*

# How We Wrote This Book

We are twenty kids between the ages of 11 and 14 who live in the Boston area and are a part of a class called The Unit at the Fayerweather Street School in Cambridge, Massachusetts. We wrote this book because the issue of divorce has affected each of us in some way. Fourteen of us have actually gone through the whole process of a divorce in our families. The rest of us still live with both our parents, but we have had fears and fantasies about divorce happening in our families or we have friends who have gone through it all.

Those of us who have gone through divorce now live in many different kinds of arrangements. Some of us live with our mothers and our brothers and sisters. Others of us live half of the time with our dads and half of the time with our moms. A few of us live with one of our parents and a stepparent. In addition we live in a large variety of homes—from inner-city apartments, to suburban houses, to rural farmhouses. Some of us have fathers who live far away—out of Massachusetts, even out of this country.

We started the work which led up to this book in the fall of 1978. Our teachers saw that the majority of us had parents who were divorced and that we had important feelings about this that were unresolved. The teachers felt that these feelings should be discussed, so we held regular discussion groups that met twice a week for about six weeks. Each group had nine people; two people did not participate in these discussions because they felt they could not discuss out loud their parents' divorce.

The teachers facilitated the groups, but we all had a say in what we discussed. We talked about our feelings and thoughts about divorce, our specific living situations, custody arrangements, parents' boyfriends or girlfriends, how we were first told about the divorce, and if divorce changed us. Sometimes kids whose parents weren't divorced felt different or left out, but we soon realized that even if parents never become divorced, the fear of divorce is a part of every child's life. That's why, today, divorce is an issue for everyone.

The two groups joined together, finally, into one big group, which met over a two week period. We all talked about some of the things which had come up in the two groups. Our teacher suggested that we read books about divorce. Most of us read a book or two — some fiction, some nonfiction — and wrote reports on what we read. Afterward we got together to talk about the books. In general we found that we had some problems with most of them. The fiction books were the best, but they were sometimes too different from our real life situations and dealt only with the obvious issues of divorce. The nonfiction books were usually written by doctors or psychiatrists or people like that; some of them had a real bias toward adults. Sometimes issues that we thought were very important, like little brothers and sisters, weren't included at all. And some of the adults who wrote these books talked down to kids like we were jerks: In general we were not happy with the books that we read.

So our teachers came up with the idea of writing a book about divorce for kids *by* kids. We talked about this idea a lot and we thought about what we'd have to do to write it. After a lot of discussion, we decided to do it. This was right before our winter vacation.

We knew we had to interview people to find out about different perspectives on divorce: kids, parents, marriage counselors, grandparents, rabbis, ministers, lawyers, teachers, divorce experts, psychiatrists. When we had finished most of the interviews, we got together as a group and discussed how to organize the book. Then we broke into teams of two or three and each team took a chapter to write. Once the first half of the book was written, parents and friends in the school typed it. We started the second half of the book the same way, though some of the writing groups were different. Everyone in the class wrote some part of the book.

When the book was finished we edited it and took photographs and drew pictures. We also worked as a class to learn about the way to find a publisher for the book. Once we found our publisher we worked with them to finalize the book, plan the way the book looks, and discuss how to promote the book. The entire process—from writing the book through publishing it—took two years.

*Sophie Aikman*
*Martin Albert*
*Matthew Allison*
*Steffi Cohen*
*Peter Corey*
*Louis Crosier*
*Regan Day*
*Sophie Gebhardt*
*Hannah Gittleman*
*Beth Hammer*
*Michael Kearney*
*Denise Lewis*
*Heather Murphy*
*Jenny Perrelli*
*Thomas Rasmussen*
*Hannah Soparkar*
*Laura Spiro*
*Sarah Steele*
*Jon Tupta*
*Adam Wolf*

# Preface

*by Eric E. Rofes, head teacher,*
*The Unit at Fayerweather Street School*

As a schoolteacher I have a commitment to wiping out ignorance. This may involve helping a child improve his or her reading skills, teaching spelling rules, or explaining how division of fractions works. It also involves helping young people come to grips with the reality of the modern world. To do this I provide my students with information and resources and help them cope with their thoughts and feelings on many issues.

Divorce is a fact of life for all families today. When I was growing up in the suburbs of Long Island I had comparatively little awareness of what divorce was about. I did not know anyone in my town who had divorced parents, and kids from what were then called "broken homes" bore a tremendous burden and stigma. Today divorce is a fact of life in every community, and children regularly struggle to come to terms with its role in their lives. Even if a child's parents do not separate or divorce, the fear of divorce can be present whenever parents have serious fights. This fear needs to be addressed. Most children have friends or classmates who have gone through divorce, and if they are to help peers through this difficult process, they need to be given the informational tools to allow them to provide comfort and support.

Schools can play an important role in helping children to understand the divorce process and to deal with their feelings. Yet many teachers are uncomfortable with this subject, and many schools feel it is an inappropriate subject to discuss in the classroom. Each teacher and each school will have to decide for itself if it will help children cope with divorce, and if so, in what manner.

I have taught before in a school where divorce was a subject that was not to be acknowledged with the class. One situation I can remember that was particularly upsetting to me was when a boy I worked with began to behave in a manner that I found unusual for him. Other children in the class began to have problems with their friend who had formerly been a very cooperative and popular person in the class. When I brought my concerns to an administrator, I was informed that the boy's parents had separated and his father had moved out of the house. This piece of information helped me to understand a lot of the boy's behavior and I expressed the desire to talk with him about the situation. I was informed that that would be "unprofessional" for me to do, and that the personal situation of this boy's family was not my concern. Furthermore, I was not permitted to encourage this boy to explain his situation to his friends, and therefore allow them to understand his changed behavior and help him cope with the separation. I became frustrated and angry. I felt I was not meeting an important responsibility and commitment I had assumed when I became a teacher.

When I first arrived at the Fayerweather Street School I was immediately impressed by the commitment the school had to addressing the full range of the children's needs. The school seemed to be centered around the children, and the young people in my class seemed self-assured, happy, and well rounded. At Fayerweather, an unusual amount of time and energy seemed to be focused on interpersonal relationships; the children appeared to be quite skilled at resolving their conflicts and disputes. During my first weeks at the school, however, I did notice that many of the children had unresolved feelings about divorce. Often these feelings came out in jest, or in off-the-cuff remarks during informal conversations; sometimes they arose in class meetings. As a teacher, I experienced much confusion and insecurity; here were kids who openly dealt with crucial life issues, yet, when the situation was directly confronting me, I felt unprepared to help them. I was nervous about how the school's administration and the children's parents would react.

I discussed this with the head of the school and she shared my observation that the children had unresolved feelings about divorce and that it was a good idea for us to deal with these feelings with the class. This was the start of the regular class discussion groups about divorce that grew into this book. After I talked with the head of the school, I realized that Fayerweather was different from my previous school; it was willing to take risks and deal with issues that were potentially controversial. Several of the parents initially did not want their children involved in the discussion, fearing that it would bring up painful feelings again. The school's administration worked closely with me to convince parents of the importance of this project and of the need for their cooperation and support. Schools and parents may not always agree, but it is crucial that they work together with the best interests of the child in mind.

Through the two-year process of writing, editing, and publishing this book, I have had a great deal of exposure to kids' feelings about divorce. I am more convinced than when we began that schools can help children cope with their feelings. Yet many teachers have reservations about dealing with divorce in the classroom, particularly with young children. They feel that childhood should be a time of innocent pleasures and enjoyment and that a discussion of divorce would blemish the beauty of childhood. There are certainly some children whose lives seem to be carefree. But by believing that most children are this way, one ignores the vast range of experiences children face in our modern world; and one fails to address the real concerns of many children. Even in a class that has only one or two children from divorced families, by failing to address divorce openly the teacher must accept responsibility for continuing to make these children feel shamed, unacceptable, and handicapped. While some teachers might feel that discussing divorce in the classroom makes divorced kids feel embarrassed and "different," the fact is that these children already feel singled out. A frank, sensitive discussion of the issue will bring divorce out into the open, make the issue a valid topic of conversation, and acknowledge families split by divorce as legitimate family units.

When I first began work on this subject with children, I felt nervous because I had had little experience with divorce. To prepare myself I did a large amount of reading and personally spoke with friends and acquaintances who had been through divorce. Still, I was not fully prepared to deal with some of the issues that came up, as well as some of the powerful feelings about my own childhood that were stirred up. Schools committed to helping children cope with divorce should be prepared to provide training sessions for all staff members. These training sessions would provide schoolteachers with up-to-date information about divorce, make them sensitive to the aspects of divorce that most concern kids, and teach counseling and discussion facilitation technique. During these sessions, teachers would have the opportunity to discuss their personal feelings about divorce and work through some of their biases and apprehensions.

Some schools have developed a variety of resources to help children deal with divorce. Extracurricular clubs like the Lexington High Divorced Kids Group (see page 61) are a place where children of divorce can get together and work on their feelings and help each other understand the implications and effects of divorce. One teacher I know has read novels dealing with the theme of divorce with her class and this has been a good way for the students to begin to probe their feelings. There are many books available to children, from toddlers through teenagers, and they should find their way into every classroom. Another teacher has integrated the issue of divorce into her course on human relations, and kids safely discuss their attitudes and experiences with divorce in a classroom. Creative teaching techniques will allow many teachers to develop a way of integrating divorce into the curriculum in a way that is appropriate to the children.

This book is intended for use by a wide variety of people. The kids who wrote the book deliberately wrote about divorce to fill what they saw as a void in the children's literature on the subject: There was no book that fully addressed the issues as they relate to kids. Furthermore, they felt that when some of them had experienced their parents' divorce, what they needed most was to speak with other kids. Adults tried to be helpful to them, but adult contact wasn't always what they needed at the time. A book about divorce, told *by* kids, *for* kids, would be particularly helpful and important.

The book will also be used by adults. Since communication between parent and child is not always at its best during divorce, this book can help educate parents about issues and concerns their child may not be able to express. Teachers who read the book will gain a greater understanding of their students and the effect that divorce may have on children. Finally, professionals involved in divorce—lawyers, counselors, judges—will learn something about how their tasks affect children and may become more sensitive to the role that children should be able to take in dealing with issues such as custody and living arrangements.

Ideally I believe this will be a book for parents to read with their children. There are many parts of this book that will make a good topic for parent-child discussion, and individual families will find that different parts of the book relate best to their individual situation. Using the book could be a safe way to delve into the subject; in this way I see the book as a tool to facilitate communication between parent and child. Some kids may resist this and prefer to have their parents read the book independently and not discuss it with them. The individual child's wishes and needs should both be looked at and respected, but the ultimate goal of this book is to make children feel more comfortable with divorce and enhance the ability of families to remain nurturing units to children throughout the divorce process.

# Acknowledgments

We interviewed many people for this book because we wanted to be sure to include a variety of perspectives on the subject of divorce. These people were valuable resources for us and include children of divorce, divorced parents, friends of divorced people, counselors, ministers and rabbis, lawyers and judges, schoolteachers, and writers. We'd like to thank Bill Aibel, Dr. William Ackerly, Jason Atwood, Bob Bell, Sue Butler, Chad Dobson, Emily Friedan, Sarah Fujiwara, Judge Edward Ginsburg, Rabbi Earl Grollman, Chris Hamilton, Larry Hill, Marsha Hiller, Jamie Keshet, Aaron Marcu, Christy Murphy, Wendi Quest, Jennifer Quest-Stern, Bernard Rogovin, Mindy Sobota, Adelaide Sproul, denise [sic] Steele, Jeanie Tibbils, Jerry Weinstein. There were many other children and adults interviewed and we thank them all for their help with this book.

We also appreciate the advice and support we received from the following groups: the Lexington High School Divorced Kids Group, the Cambridge Divorce and Mediation Center, the Board of Directors of the Fayerweather Street School, and Steve Hurwitz and the Bureau of the Census. We'd like to thank the following members of the Fayerweather Street School community for their help in typing and copying the manuscripts: Phyllis Cohen, Jon Spector, the Soparkar family, Peter Gebhardt, and Olivia Fiske. Linda Brown has been a very valuable person to us in the research, typing, and production of the manuscript.

John Irving, Alex Humez, Elizabeth Foote-Smith, and Sasha Allison helped us learn about the process of publishing a book. People who read the manuscript and helped us improve the text include our parents, Sarah Benet and Shippen Page of the Massachusetts Committee for Children and Youth, and feminist lawyer Katherine Triantifillou. Dick Derry and Amanda Cole are kids from the Unit class of 1980 who drew additional drawings for the book.

Finally, we'd like to thank the teachers at Fayerweather Street School who guided this project: Len Gittleman, who is credited with the idea for the book a year before we actually began to deal with the issue of divorce; Willy Williams and Alison Milburn, who aided our efforts; Sue Pease, who conducted some of our initial rap groups and helped us with planning and writing the book; and Eric Rofes, who coordinated the entire project from start to finish and kept the book alive through the difficult process of discussing our feelings, researching the subject, writing, editing, rewriting, and publishing.

# *1*

# *Different Kinds of Families*

The traditional nuclear family consists of a mother, a father, a boy, a girl, and, of course, Willy the dog. The mother spends her day at home, baking brownies for her children's afterschool snack or maybe doing the ironing. The children, meanwhile, are at school. When they arrive home they are greeted by their mother with a plate of warm brownies. After their little snack they go to their rooms and do their homework. Dad is at work at the hardware store all day. When he gets home he sits down in an overstuffed chair and reads the evening paper. On Saturdays the father and son go fishing, while mother and daughter stay home and cook. When the father and son get back they are greeted by a kiss on the cheek and a burning pipe for father. And Willy the dog comes trotting in the door after them.

Our families were never like this. To tell you the truth, we don't know of any family who is. Do you?

These are some of the differences between our families and the traditional nuclear family:

Willy, the dog: a
member of every
traditional nuclear family.

- Our mothers aren't housewives.
- Our mothers don't slave over a hot stove all day.
- Our fathers don't always have time to take us fishing.
- Our parents don't live together any more.

An extended family includes other close relatives such as grandparents, uncles, or aunts who live with the nuclear family. Television's Waltons are this type of family: They have five kids, a mother, a father, and grandparents. The grandparents living with them makes them an *extended* family. Another example is on the television show *My Three Sons:* The Douglas family could be considered to be an extended family because their uncle lives with them, although there is no mother in the Douglas home.

A hundred years ago, most people lived in extended families and kids grew up very close to grandparents, aunts, and uncles. Some families still live this way. The extended family remains a major way of living in parts of Europe and Asia. In our school we have a family who live in an extended family. Debbie and Bruce live with their mother, their grandparents, and their uncle. They have a lot more contact with their relatives than many of us who live only with our parents and siblings.

Aside from nuclear and extended families, there are many other variations. Sarah lives with her mother and her sister in what is called a single-parent family. Regan lives with her mother and stepfather, another kind of family. Sophie Aikman lives with her mother and

Having grandparents in your extended family can have many benefits for the kids.

several other adults in an almost communal situation. In addition to these types of families, we know kids living in foster homes and in two-family homes (where two single-parent families are living together to save money and share a household).

Catherine lives in a complicated type of family that we have named the "Gitts and Gurks." This is when two people, both divorced, are living together. Mr. Gurk and Ms. Gitts each have their kids visit at the house at one time or another, and the rest of the time both sets of kids are at their other parent's house. So at one point the couple are alone; at another time Mr. Gurk's kids are there; at still another time Ms. Gitts' kids are there; and sometimes they're all there. While this seems very complicated, many people live this way and enjoy the changes.

Most people have the idea that a nuclear family is problem-free and that life comes more easily to them than to some of these more complex types of family. We don't agree. This is not to say that nuclear families are full of problems, but they have their share.

Many people grew up believing that a nuclear family is the best kind of family to be in.

Regan remembers, "When I was about eight years old I had a friend, Lori Johnson, who I thought had the perfect life in a 'perfect nuclear family,' though I didn't call the situation 'nuclear' at the time. Lori seemed to have everything that I didn't have (with the exception of brothers, which I had)—a swimming pool, Madame Alexander dolls, lots of expensive clothes, and lots of sweets. I noticed, though, that she didn't have the mental knowledge that I had from the emotional experience of my parents' divorce and the background of having brothers. Still, I felt that my family wasn't the perfect American family that her's was."

Linda Brown, an administrator in our school, told us about how she felt when her divorce happened: "When I first got divorced I hated to think of the empty place setting at the end of the table, because it felt like the family wasn't whole anymore. My son and I had to make the transition to feeling that a single-parent family is just as 'whole' as a nuclear family."

Steven Hurwitz of the Bureau of the Census told us that in 1976

A nuclear family.

the National Center for Health Statistics showed that there were 1,083,000 divorces and there were a total of 1,117,000 kids involved in these divorces. In 1977, there were 1,091,000 divorces and 1,095,000 kids were affected. He estimated that in 1978, out of all the families with kids, 18.9 percent of them lived in single-parent homes and 81.1 percent lived in two-parent homes. This indicates to us that more and more kids are experiencing divorce, and many kids will live in single-parent homes for at least part of their childhood.

There are several reasons why people grow up to believe that nuclear families are so perfect:

*Television shows:* For example, consider the Cunninghams on the television show *Happy Days.* There is a mother who is a housewife, a father who works, a boy and a girl. They live in a nuclear family. They're happy!

*Commercials:* Television commercials often show a mother serving bacon and eggs to her smiling husband and kids. They look like a happy family, right? They're nuclear!

*People:* The Jones family across the street are nuclear. They look happy. Actually all you can see is the kids playing ball and going on trips with the parents, right? You can't see the fights over using the bathroom or the arguments over who has to clean up after the puppy.

Is it possible that the Jones family are no happier than you or me? We are mostly kids from divorced families who now live in different kinds of families. We have these memories and/or fantasies about nuclear families:

- They look like pictures in magazines.
- We imagine a mother, father, and kids building a tree house.
- The nuclear family is very close.
- We are reminded of four people standing in front of a yellow house with a picket fence and roses.
- We think of going bowling together.

What are your memories/fantasies? Are they like ours? Do you remember when you lived in a "perfect" family? Do you remember when "perfection" started to end?

Chapter **2**

# War in the Household

Everybody fights: Kids fight, animals fight, friends fight, so parents have the same right to fight. Sometimes, however, we wonder what causes our parents to fight.

Parents argue for many reasons, including big-decision fights like "Who's going to take care of the child, you or me?"; silly, unimportant arguments like "You're squeezing the toothpaste the wrong way"; or even fights like "Who's going to take the laundry to the cleaners today?"

No type of fighting is really right or wrong, and the reasons *themselves* aren't right or wrong. It's the feelings *behind* the reasons that are important.

These feelings can include anger, frustration, loneliness, and sometimes even jealousy. A fight could be caused by two people just plain disliking each other or just not appealing to each other anymore. In silly, seemingly unimportant fights, people are sometimes dealing with serious issues. Just because people are talking about the laundry it doesn't mean that that argument is about the laundry; it could be about the feelings lined up with who does the laundry, or totally unrelated feelings and the laundry is an excuse to argue.

If you live in a house with constant fighting, you know the signs of a fight beginning:

- voices rising, becoming harsher and more shrill, eyes narrowing, bodies becoming tense;
- people throwing things;
- slamming doors;
- someone not paying attention or ignoring another person.

When these signs start to show up, you may want to excuse yourself and leave!

If you live in a house for a long time with constant fighting, you will also see the different styles of fighting. Some fighting is noisy and some is quiet, depending on the kinds of people. There are big fights and little ones. A big fight is the most violent. A big fight involves greater feelings than a small fight.

A student in our school wrote about little fights:

> My mother used to go out with a man named Jim. Whenever they got into fights it was usually for stupid reasons. The main reason was bacon. My mother and I liked bacon nice and flimsy. But Jim and his kids liked it very crisp and almost burnt. A lot of the fights happened at breakfast because Jim's kids would complain about everything they could see. Then they would sing and jump around. While all this is happening, my mother is making her flimsy bacon. When she would bring the bacon to the table, they would start crying because it wasn't good enough for them. When it gets that hectic is when the fighting usually starts. I think all the fighting is why they broke up!

The physical fights are the worst kinds of fights and the kids should definitely walk out of the room when they begin. Another student in our school wrote:

One night five years ago when I lived in Belmont I had just gone to bed and wasn't quite asleep when I heard my mother and her boyfriend having a fight. This of course was terrible because me being only eight years old, hearing this crazy yelling was so scary. I must have thought they would kill each other. The next thing I heard was the front door slam. The next morning when I left for school, I saw the screen door was ripped from the hinges.

Hitting mothers and kids is not very good, especially kids, because parents are much bigger than kids and much stronger. As far as a man hitting a mother, it is not good at all, but a mother can sometimes retaliate better than a kid. If it's physical violence, it is not good for *everybody*. If a kid sees a fight going on between parents he or she should walk out.

There is also something called a silent fight. We don't think very many parents do it. Silent fighting is when parents don't actually hit each other or throw things, but don't cooperate either. They do little things to annoy each other, like not listening, or leaving things undone.

What can you do? Not much, but try not to annoy your parents or ask questions while they're fighting, or they might get mad and start arguing about you or to you.

Family fights can be caused by some very simple things — like bacon.

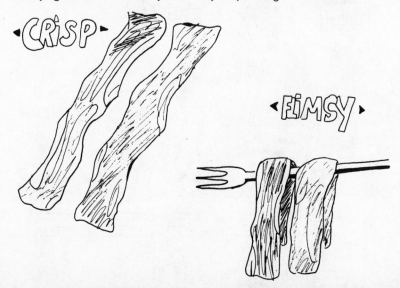

Some kids do different things during fighting between their parents: One seven-year-old girl said, "I would usually run up to my room and hide under my bed." Another girl said, "I would try to make one of them wake up early and let the other one sleep so they wouldn't fight. It worked sometimes!" And a five-year-old boy was glad that his parents got divorced because when they were married, "I just kept on hearing them yell."

Reactions to fighting are different; it all depends on the person listening to the fight. Younger kids don't seem to talk about fights as much as older kids, but they show their anger or fear in some other way. Older kids are more verbal (talkative) than younger kids. They talk more because they understand more.

We hope you're not in a situation where lots of fights are happening, but if things get so bad that you want to run away, then talk to one or both of your parents or an aunt or uncle or any other relative or friend that you're close to. Believe it or not, your parents might have wanted

When things get bad you may want to talk with a relative.

Writing in a journal is a good way to let your feelings out.

to run away when they were your age, too, so they may understand your feelings. In most movies or books about divorce the family is fairly close. We're afraid this is not always true, and it may not be true in your case. If it isn't, you should find close friends and talk to them about your parents' fighting.

One student in our school told us, "I was only seven when my parents separated and no one told me anything." People should tell you what's going on when big changes are happening. In fact, if they don't tell you, you should ask what's happening. Go right up and ask them. It might be scary, but ask your parents and try not to ask in the middle of an argument. Remember, one of the most important things to do during a war in the household is to talk to someone, anyone, about your feelings.

If you don't think that you can talk to anyone about the fights, not even your friends, then what you should do is write. Write a book, a diary, a poem or many poems about your parents. This will get your feelings out (and in the end your writing could even get published).

A common question asked by kids when their parents are fighting is, "Is it my fault that my parents fight?"

The answer is "No." It is almost never your fault. Although fights happen in all homes and in all families, the reasons differ from family to family, just as the reactions to parents fighting differ from kid to kid.

Common feelings which kids have when parents fight include fear, anger, embarrassment, insecurity, and disappointment.

## Fear

"I woke up in the middle of the night all the time to my parents screaming at one another," said twelve-year-old Derek. "My stomach would tie up in knots and I'd feel like throwing up. My heartbeat would speed up because I was so scared. I don't know why I was so scared."

Kids feel scared when parents fight, mostly because either they don't know what will happen afterwards or they're not used to parents being so violent toward one another. "It's like going to the dentist," said fourteen-year-old Alex. "You just want it to be over. One time I was so anxious I just yelled down the stairs 'When will this *stop!*' "

Thirteen-year-old Marlene said, "I was cleaning the house after school and my parents weren't home. Suddenly they both burst in yelling. I was furious! There I was doing them a favor by cleaning the house and they just burst in and scared me and made me feel really horrified."

## Anger

Kids often feel angry when their parents fight. Sometimes this anger is directed toward their parents for being, as Laura says, "inconsiderate, self-indulgent, and childish." Sometimes, on the other hand, this anger is directed toward themselves. This is when they feel that their parent's fighting is their fault. Ten-year-old Chet said, "I get real mad, 'cause they do it right in front of me! I wish they'd do it when I'm not there!" Thirteen-year-old Tony told us, "Even though I know it's not that way, I can't help feeling like I'm the cause of all their fights."

## Embarrassment

Twelve-year-old Donna told us, "One time, my friend was sleeping over and my dad and stepmother got into a fight. I could have died! They were arguing about *sex!* My friend pretended she didn't notice. I was so embarrassed!"

This is a really embarrassing situation to be in. You don't know what your friend is thinking. Another problem is worrying about neighbors hearing the fights (if it gets to that noise level). Twelve-year-old Consuelo said, "I was sure the neighbors heard everything. The next day it seemed like everyone was staring at my mother."

## Insecurity

"Last time my parents fought, they were fighting about who would spend the weekend at home with me. Neither one of them wanted to! That's when I felt insecure," said Kelly, a fifteen-year-old boy from New York. During a fight between parents, kids occasionally feel insecure, almost always because they worry about what will happen to them (which they shouldn't worry about anyway). Cindy, a nine-year-old girl, said, "When they fight, I feel like they're forgetting all about me. What if they both just left?"

## Disappointment

Poochie, an eleven-year-old boy, said, "When I first heard my parents fighting I felt very sad because it seems like that's a cheap thing to do. They're not always that kind of people. I was very disappointed in the both of them. They were acting like babies."

Fear.

Embarrassment.

Insecurity.

Anger.

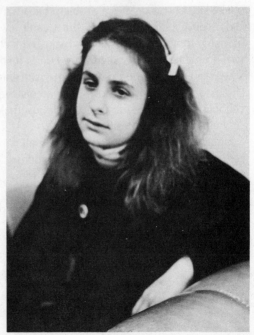

Kids sometimes feel disappointed in their parents for fighting. They shouldn't feel this way. As we've said before, everyone fights.

Many people think that people fight because they hate each other. This is seldom true. A lot of parents fight because they love each other and want to work out their differences. It's just hard sometimes to do this without getting a little loud. If they hated each other, why would they bother trying to work it out?

A scary thing for bigger kids as well as little kids is when parents yell at them. This yelling can be about anything from not washing out your cup to setting the house on fire. No matter what it's about or how loud it gets, your parents still love you. *They do not yell because they hate you.* A few reasons that parents yell at kids are (a) because they are upset with the kid; (b) because they are upset with themselves; (c) because they are upset with someone else; (d) because they are frustrated.

Something that happens to a lot of kids is their parents asking them to take sides. This creates a problem because, as one boy in our class said, "I love both my parents but I can't always agree with both of them. My mother used to always make me feel like I had to agree with her. No matter who I agreed with, one of them would be mad at me. Now I say, 'Please don't involve me with this because it's not fair.' Things are working out now. My parents really understand." Never feel obligated to take sides. You could just make it clear that you don't like being put in that position.

Fights happen in all homes and with all families. They are different from a full-scale war. War in the house doesn't just mean an argument —it means several long arguments. It's more like a war without weapons, something that goes on and on, grows deeper and deeper until thoughts of a "separation" start to come in and out of people's minds.

Chapter **3**

# *The Decision to Separate*

A dish flew through the living room and hit the wall next to Charles. Charles said, "What are you trying to do — kill me or something?"

"I only wish!" Jane said.

That was the beginning of the *decision to separate!*

"I want a divorce," said Jane to Charles.

"But why, honey? Why?" Charles looked confused.

"We're not getting along. You're away too much. You don't care about me anymore." Jane looked upset about what she had just said.

"Well that's fine with me, I'll give you a few reasons why I want a divorce." Then he went and sat on the couch with Jane across from him in the rocking chair.

"There's no money in this family but you refuse to get a job. I don't like the way the children are being raised. You have no respect for me either (and a wife should have respect for her husband)." Then he stood up and pointed at Jane. "I don't like the school the children are going to." He started to shout. "I have my suspicions about you." Then he sat back down on the couch.

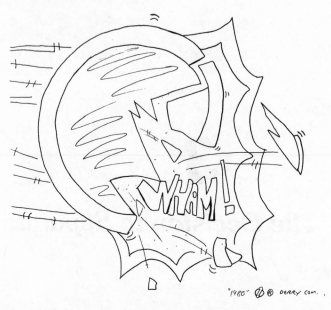

"1980" Ⓓ Ⓡ DERRY COM.

"I've been true to you since the day we were married. Never once did I think about cheating on you but I've my doubts about how true you've been to me." Jane was on the verge of tears. But she was glad she said what she did.

Jane continued, "Alright, let's talk about this like human beings. I feel that the kids and I can make it with the help of a little money. You can see them any time you want to."

"You, Jane? Why should you get to take my kids away from me? Why should you be able to take the kids?"

"Alright, do you think we should get separated Charles?"

"Yes, I think we should get separated. Jane, why don't we send the kids to grandmother's house while we work out who gets custody of the kids?"

"Now *that's* the first good idea you've had all day."

This story is only a soap opera version of a decision to separate. One of the things we wanted you to know in this story is the conflict the kids sometimes cause in the decision to separate. This story contains some of the reasons parents think about separation, such as money, no respect, arguments over children.

One of the seven-year-old children we interviewed, Mindy Sobota, spoke to us about why she thinks her parents first got separated: "My mother didn't like getting in fights with my father all the time. They weren't happy living together anymore."

Jason Atwood, a six-year-old child, told us why he thinks his parents got divorced: "They were yelling and screaming all the time and my mother wanted to live in the city and my father wanted to live in the country."

Larry Hill, a marriage counselor, gave three major causes for separations:

- Parents can't be together in pleasant ways.
- People expect too much from a marriage.
- People expect marriage to be an answer to all their problems, but marriage is not a problem solver.

Being a marriage counselor, Larry Hill experiences a lot of separations. Coping with separations is a very complicated problem these days. In our opinion, separation is an unsure thing and people are very unsure about what will happen. A lot of uncomfortable feelings come out in the open, and the decision to separate is just one of those.

The decision to separate can come suddenly, gradually, or after long discussions. Paul, a fourteen-year-old boy, experienced the decision of his parents to separate as a quick decision and this raised many different reactions and emotions in him. He told us, "When my parents and I were eating dinner one evening they told me about their decision. Right out of the blue they said that they were getting separated and dad was moving out tomorrow. I was horrified, since I had seen no signs leading up to this, and I resented them strongly for hiding so much from me. I tried to discuss it with them and to understand what was going on, but they were very bitter toward each other and didn't seem to care what I thought at that point. I still don't know the reasons for the separation or the eventual divorce that was final two weeks ago. It's still confusing for me."

Sue's situation, unlike Paul's, was a gradual one. Eleven-year-old Sue explains, "About four months ago I noticed when my parents were together that they seemed sort of cold and mean towards each other. That made me feel awkward and sad. It kept getting worse and I would ask them what was wrong, and they would just say 'Mommy and Daddy just aren't getting along right now, dear' and leave it at that. I knew what separation and divorce were when two months later they discussed it with me. My father moved out a week after the discussion and they're getting a divorce now. I don't feel too bad about it because they were so unhappy together and that made me sad. I guess it's better now that they're getting divorced, but I don't like the split custody idea."

Another situation different from Paul and Sue's situations is David's. He went through a long, detailed process with his parents before they decided to separate. At the time, David was thirteen years old. He told us, "My parents first mentioned separation to me about two years ago and completely explained the whole situation. At first I panicked, thinking my father would leave and I would never see him again; or my mother would leave or maybe one of them was having an affair, but none of that was true. They explained that their marriage just wasn't working out as they thought it would and that a separation might be better. It seemed as though they talked for months before the actual decision was made. I guess they were very concerned about my feelings and views. I think my situation with my parents turned out the most civilized of all my friends' parents' divorces."

Most of the separations we've seen end up in divorce. But out of the few we've seen that do stay together we think they end up staying together longer than if they hadn't gone through a separation. A couple of reasons why this might be so is that maybe when the people were living apart they realized how much they really loved each other. Or maybe they worked out some of the problems they were having.

Something most kids don't realize is that the decision to separate is very hard for the parents as well as for the kids. It's a decision that will affect them emotionally, but in the olden days it used to affect them socially as well. Divorced people were seen as "different," "sinful," or "bad."

How could two people who loved each other very much, suddenly stop loving one another so much that they could get divorced over it? How could two people who loved one another so much to get married stop loving one another and keep fighting and carrying on? Why didn't they say to themselves when they married, "Will this end up in a divorce or will it work out alright?"

These are some of the questions kids wonder about. They're not, however, questions anyone, even the parents, can answer.

When parents are going through a separation one of the main reasons they think of staying together is the kids. Some of the people we interviewed seem to have almost the same feelings when it comes to parents staying together for the kids' sake. Dr. William Ackerly, a child psychologist, told us that he really feels that parents often stay in an unhappy situation only for the child's sake. In fact he had a client whose parents were staying together for her sake and she told him that she wished her parents would get separated for her sake, because they were making life miserable for her.

The time of the decision to separate is a very emotional time. Some parents send their kid to grandma's house while they're working things out. Some couples can get back together, but a lot don't. In some separations, the two people aren't friends at all. We have also known people who were separated, yet remained good friends.

When parents are getting separated, kids get worried and confused. But separation isn't all that bad when it's over. Sometimes if you talk to your parents or brothers and sisters it might help you get through a separation.

Kids of all ages have a hard time when parents are getting separated, but we think it's the hardest for kids between the ages of five and eight. Some of the reasons for this are because when you're that young it's very hard to understand what's going on, and it's also pretty hard for you to make the transitions from one parent to another. It's hard for you to accept the fact that your parents are getting separated.

## *Telling the Kids*

If parents decide to go ahead and get divorced, telling the kids is probably one of the most difficult parts of a divorce. There are many reasons why this is such a difficult matter:

- Parents might not be getting along too well due to the fact that things aren't going too well between them.
- Fights that parents might be having could make it hard for them to talk to you together. They might fight over how to tell you.
- It will also be very hard for your parents to deal with the fact that they are finally getting a divorce.
- Parents may be feeling guilty due to the fact that they might not have told you sooner or because of what the divorce will cause you to feel.
- Another reason that telling the kids might be difficult might be that the parents are embarrassed because they might feel as though they failed in their marriage or failed their children.
- Your parents may approach the subject of divorce in an off-the-subject fashion, thus causing you further confusion. They may do this because they don't want to hurt you.

Telling the kids.

You might be thinking that your parents are neglecting you; but remember that getting a divorce is probably a hard thing for your parents to do, and they probably need to put most of their time and energy into their own problems. Also, they are so worried about hurting you that they may put it off.

## When Kids Should Be Told

Time is a very important factor in a divorce. As soon as parents find out that the separation or divorce is going to happen they should tell their kids about it. We would have much more respect for parents and their actions if they told their kids about the divorce as soon as they knew, rather than days later.

Most of the kids we talked to said if they had found out about their parents' divorce before their parents told them, they would feel very mad at them. It's every kid's right to know what's going to happen in their life.

One thirteen-year-old girl told us:

> I came home from school one day last fall and found that my mother wasn't home. This was unusual. My father was sitting at the kitchen table, talking to my older brother, and when I entered the room they fell silent and looked at me with long, serious faces. I made a couple of jokes, but it was obvious it was no joking matter. Then they hit me with it: My parents were getting divorced.
>
> "Are you kidding?? What the hell do you and mom think you're doing, just deciding to get divorced, huh??" I said in a high-pitched voice to my father.
>
> "Shut up, Katie, and listen," my older brother Tom replied.
>
> My father took over from there and explained that mom and he had decided to get divorced about two months ago, and a fight they had had earlier today set off the separation and "bye-bye mom." My stomach churned as it always does when I'm upset, and I bit my nails feverishly. I was furious with resentment and

anger that they hadn't told me earlier. I felt as though I had been denied of the information that formed my future.

Though I still resent my parents for not telling me, I now see their reasons for their actions. That makes it a little easier.

## How Kids Should Be Told

Some of the kids we have talked to feel that parents should be careful in the way they tell their kids about separation or divorce. If kids are told about these sensitive issues in the wrong way, it could lead to a lot of uncomfortable feelings.

If there are several kids in the family it might be a good idea to tell them all together, even if there is a large age difference. This is because it would be hard for most of the kids we know to contain this information if they were told alone. Divorce is a hard secret to keep.

It also would not be fair to other kids in the family if they were told after one of their brothers or sisters. The kid that had been told would feel very mad at everything and his or her siblings would not know what was going on. We also think that all kids have the right to know about the divorce or separation at the same time.

Younger kids might not understand everything they are told about divorce or separation. It would be the older kid's job to help them understand. The older kid would probably like time alone with his or her parents to talk to them about the issues involved. Then he or she could help their younger brothers or sisters.

It is important for kids to be told truthfully about what is going on. Some parents choose to tell their kids in a very direct and blunt manner, explaining things thoroughly and making sure the children understand. The parents may also choose to spend time with the kids when they're sad, to comfort them, and attempt to piece out the confusion. This style of telling the children is a good one; helping the kids through all steps of divorce is an important matter.

Other parents may choose to tell their children the absolute bare facts, possibly leaving the children confused, unless they choose not

Big brothers can be a big help explaining what's going on to younger brothers.

to want to hear of excessive details. This style of telling the kids is not the best way for many families. It can cause lack of communication between family members and frequent fighting between relatives and people outside the family.

Some kids would like to be told almost everything about what's going on between their parents. Other kids prefer *not* to hear anything.

Judy Russ, nine years old, reacted to her parents' divorce in a negative way and became very cold to them. She made a decision that many children make when their parents get divorced. This is what she told us: "When my parents decided to get divorced I told them they were making a big mistake. They tried to explain why they were going ahead with the divorce, but I told them I didn't want to hear anything about anything. All I wanted to know was where my dad was moving and when I was allowed to see him. I didn't talk to my parents very much for about two weeks after they told me, but I'm okay now and I see my dad every weekend. I don't ever want to know why they divorced, I just don't care to know."

Sam Ale, fifteen years old, told us that he felt much different than Judy about his parents' divorce. "I was eager to know everything about their divorce, when they made the final decision last year. They didn't go through a separation period, the divorce was just a decision they made over a two week period, involving discussions with me and a

## ALL KIDS NEED TO KNOW THESE THINGS

All kids need to be told the following things about the divorce or separation:

- Parents don't love each other but they still love their kids.
- Life may be very hard before parents reach settlement.
- Where the kids are going to live.
- How often will the kids see their parents.
- Why their parents are splitting unless the reason was very harsh (like an affair, or something that had nothing to do with the kids' life).

marriage counselor, for a while. I was sort of stunned that they decided to get a divorce all of a sudden, but realized later that they had been arguing for some time. I was interested in all the steps of the divorce at the time, but particularly in the custody rights. I wanted to have a say in that. They didn't go through a big court-custody type hassle, but sat down with me and we decided together. My parents didn't understand why I was so interested in the whole ordeal, but I was and I'm glad I was because I don't feel in the dark about the subject of divorce or about my parents."

### How Kids Shouldn't Be Told

As kids, we would not want to be told it was our fault, even if it was. However, we don't know of any cases where the divorce was the kids' fault.

We would not want to be bribed with presents, when we were being told. We would feel much better receiving our parents' time and love rather than their gifts (see "Weekend Santa," pages 88–92).

It would also be very hard for us if we were told that one of our parents was having an affair with another person. One twelve-year-old girl told us:

> Right after my parents separated my dad brought me home from my mom's house and I saw this woman sitting in my dad's living room. I thought she was his secretary or something, but then he kissed her. I asked him who she was, and he said, "She's my girlfriend, Cathy. She'll be spending the night tonight." Then I asked him why and how long she had been his girlfriend. "Daddy needs close friends, Cathy," he said. "Jill has been with me for a month now, dear." I yelled real loud at him and called him an asshole, but he didn't listen. He didn't care if I hadn't known, I asked him for a reason about why he hadn't told me, but he didn't say anything. He introduced me to Jill and the first thing I said to her was "Get out of my house!" Now I like her okay, but I don't think she belongs with my dad.

We don't think that it's good if a parent tells the kids alone because that parent could make the other parent seem like the bad guy.

We think it's very important that one parent never says that it was the other parent's fault. This would most likely hurt the parent-child relationship. This is definitely not a fair thing to do to any child.

Before we started writing this book we talked a lot about truth. Parents should never lie to their kids about divorce. Parents should not tell kids mom or dad is going on a long trip. Parents shouldn't say that mom or dad will be back in a little while.

There are a lot of do's and don't's, but the most important thing is to try to be honest and direct.


## It's Not Your Fault

When you get told about separation or divorce, don't think it's your fault. It isn't your fault, or your brother's or sister's. Both of your parents probably decided this themselves because of their own prob-

You may feel like the problems your parents are having are all your fault.

lems or fights they had. You might also think that it's not really going to happen, but it probably is. You've got to deal with the fact that your parents really are going to go their separate ways. If you don't deal with that now you'll have to deal with it later, and it will probably be harder the longer you wait. The main reason it will get harder is that your parents will get further into their divorce.

One of the things that scares kids most about divorce is that they see their nuclear family breaking up and they think that other arrangements of families aren't as good. This isn't true, but most of us have felt it at one point or another.

Even in a nuclear family there are often disagreements between family members. Sometimes these disagreements can become full-scale wars, and parents might start to think about separation and divorce. Why? Because they are unhappy together. But people hesitate. This is a hard thing for parents who thought that they lived in a very happy nuclear family. They become hesitant and might avoid divorce at any expense. There are many reasons why people hesitate to get divorced:

*Religion.* Some religions say that it is not right to get divorced. The Pope has told Roman Catholics that they can't get divorced.

*Shame.* Some people are ashamed of their problems. Some people think they should never have problems.

*Fear, humiliation, embarrassment.* People are often scared that they will fail to raise their child properly without their spouse. There is often a lot of humiliation and/or embarrassment for everyone in the family who has to deal with their friends.

*Kids.* People are very much concerned about "What does it mean for us to get divorced in terms of our children?"

For many reasons, some people decide to separate and divorce. Families change a lot then.

When you're told about the change you may get angry at members of your family, like brothers, sisters, and parents. First of all, don't think that it's your siblings' fault; they've doubtless had nothing to do with it. They'll probably be upset and need support, so don't be mad at them; or, if you are, try to be as nice as possible. Don't be mad at your parents either. They're not divorcing to hurt you; they're doing it because they have to. They probably fight a lot and therefore they can't live together, so even if you're upset, try to understand that they are upset, too. Like your brothers and sisters, they'll need support, though they'll probably first need you to do chores and try not to fight.

*Chapter* **4**

# Separation: It's Not the End of the World

Your parents' separation may come as a tremendous shock to you. That's very normal. If the separation does not come as a shock to you, that's all right too. A separation means that your parents will not be living together. A separation is sometimes for the better, even though it may not seem like it at the time. If your parents aren't living together, they hopefully won't be fighting as much.

You may think that it's the end of the world because your parents are crying and fighting. Seeing parents cry can be very scary. You're probably going to feel upset because there is a lot of anger and sadness between you and your parents. It is fine if you feel upset and you cry; a divorce is very hard and painful at times and you can be upset in many ways. You can also be confused and feel you're alone, with no one to help you. You can be scared because you think that your parents are going to hurt each other. A separation may also make you sometimes embarrassed. The whole thing is very difficult

Seeing your mother crying can be an upsetting experience.

because everyone in your whole family is upset and hard to live with.

One of the best ways to deal with your feelings is to talk to a friend. You will find that a friend can help you with almost any problem. If your friend has parents who are divorced, they have probably gone through just about the same thing you're going through. Friends can tell you what to expect. If you don't talk to a friend, you should talk to someone in the family like an aunt or an uncle. They are your parents' brothers or sisters and they probably know your parents very well. Since they are about the same age as your parents, they may be able to tell you what your parents are going through.

There are also bad ways of dealing with your feelings. Don't take out your anger and hurt on other people. It may help to find some type of hobby or sports program to take your mind off the separation. You can enroll in a public sports program like Little League. You could also get into something around the house, like making candles or making things out of wood. The advantage of sports is that you can get out some of your anger by hitting balls or running. A divorce is

You may feel isolated and confused when your parents separate.

hard, but you can't let it ruin your life, your fun, and your relationships with your parents and friends.

There is one question that almost always comes up: "Do I have to tell my friends?" You could cover it up by lying whenever someone asks you where one or the other parent is. Lies usually catch up with you in the long run. You should probably tell your friends because they will be able to help you.

You have to think about where and how to tell your friends that your parents are separated. A situation may arise where a friend at school may ask you if your father or mother will drive them to a hockey game, or something similar to that. However, they don't know that one of your parents is not living at home. You could tell them right there and then that your parents are separated. You may feel like this isn't the right time. If this is so, maybe you could ask them over to your house one night and tell them.

Don't be afraid to break down and cry in front of your friends. Crying is the best way to get anger and frustration out. If your friends are true friends, they will understand and try to help you instead of laughing or acting cruel.

Ann once had a good friend whose parents had just decided to separate. Her friend called her up and said, "I really have to talk to someone." Then she started to cry. Ann didn't know what was wrong, so she really couldn't make her friend feel better. Then the crying stopped and her friend said in a really hurt voice, "My mother and father are going to separate."

Ann's parents had separated the year before so that Ann knew just how her friend felt. Then Ann told her first to calm down and asked if she wanted to come over and talk about it. Her friend said no, that they had a friend over to cheer her mother up so she couldn't leave. Ann asked her how her mother was feeling and she replied: "She's okay, but she's tired and worn out." Ann remembered how her mother had looked white and very tired and her eyes were always bloodshot. Then the conversation ended.

That is just one of the various ways you could tell your friends. Ann recalled that last year when her parents had first separated, it was easier to tell her girlfriends about the situation than it was to tell her boyfriends. Girls sometimes are able to tell each other things and boys can tell other boys.

The question about whether or not to tell your friends about your family problems may make you feel very insecure and alone.

## How to Relate to Your Parents

At first your parents might be upset, so do what you can to help them. Don't get mad at them and try not to bother them too much. Help around the house and be cooperative.

Yana is a girl whose parents were getting separated and she was very upset. She knew that she'd have to help her parents through the separation, so she helped around the house and cleaned up her room without being asked to. It was hard to get what she wanted because her mother was upset most of the time. Yana also usually had a sleep-over guest every week and another guest on Sundays. After the separation, Yana only had the Sunday guest knowing it would bother her mother less. Yana's parents became less and less upset as the days passed. Now Yana and her parents get along well. Yana has two different rooms, one at her father's house and one at her mother's. Yana's parents are still separated. Her father lives in Florida and her mother lives in Oklahoma. Yana still sees her father every so often.

There is a lot of confusion that comes with a divorce. Your mind is so busy because of all the anger and sadness. There are many different kinds of confusion. You are probably confused because you don't know if you're going to move or have to switch back and forth from your mother's to your father's house. Confusion is caused by wondering. When you don't know what is going to happen and there is a lot on your mind, you can easily get confused.

Friends can help you through the hard times.

Don't let your anger
affect your school work.

When you get confused, you start to think of your whole future and your troubles. This just confuses you more. Then you start to think of why you're scared and angry. With all of your problems on your mind, you may cry a lot. One of the questions you may have is will your parents get back together or won't they? The answer is that they probably will not. However, since there is a possibility that they *will* get back together, you will be wondering if they are going to reunite. The best way to deal with your confusion is to relax. You should think things out and organize your life. You might also want to talk to one of your parents so that they can answer some of your questions about divorce. A bad way to deal with confusion is to think of all your problems at once. This can just worry and confuse you more. Usually confusion clears up in time. Most of your problems just work themselves out.

The anger you are feeling, if you're feeling any at all, is most likely a hurt, frustrated anger. If this anger is toward your parents, you may feel that they owe you something. Maybe you feel that since your parents hurt you, you want to hurt them back. Your parents care about how you feel and don't want to hurt you, so try not to hurt them. Your parents have a lot of anger in them, too, so you must realize they also need help. The anger you are feeling may affect your school work. Try not to let it. Your work is very important and can be a good way to keep your mind off your home situation.

## The Separation Agreement

Sometimes a separation comes with a few legal agreements. Your parents may want to decide in a "complaint for separate support" when you're going to visit the two parents or who moves out of the house. Not every separation requires a document. Sometimes a parent just leaves without any written agreement.

A separation agreement is a written agreement showing who will get the property and how much money your father agrees to pay your mother or your mother agrees to pay your father. The agreement also may arrange your custody, which parent is responsible for you. Your parents have to decide where you are going to live and for how long. They have to work out your visiting the parent you are not living with.

After your parents have agreed on a settlement, they both have to sign it and so do your parents' lawyer or lawyers. Sometimes it is easier if each of your parents has a lawyer. In writing an agreement, both your parents may have to give up a little so that they can agree with each other. This is sometimes hard and gets your parents very mad at each other.

It is very important that children have some say in what goes into a separation agreement. A sample separation agreement is discussed below. It is a first draft, which means all or parts of it might change as your parents negotiate. It's from one of the families in our school. These are only parts of the agreement. When you read it you should look for places where you think that the child should have input. Every kid should read their parents' separation agreement. It will make some kids more aware of their situation and it will answer some of their questions. It will also clear up a lot of confusion and the children may trust their parents more.

## *Custody of the Minor Child*

Let's pretend that you are Caleb, the child in this separation agreement. The agreement tells you who you will live with and where you will live. It states that both parents will spend a certain amount of time with you.

The custody of the minor child, Caleb, shall be in the Wife. It is anticipated that the Wife will maintain a home for Caleb, as she does at present, and may continue to do so wherever she chooses to reside within the continental United States.

Both parents acknowledge their great love for Caleb and both are aware of the privilege and responsibility of having the child be with them. Each parent shall have the opportunity to visit with and take Caleb for reasonable lengths of time while he is in the custody of the other parent upon the giving of adequate notice and with due consideration for the other parent's existing plans. Generally, the duration and frequency of such visits shall be arranged to give both the custodial and non-custodial parent equal opportunity to be with Caleb on weekends and school vacations according to their needs and desires. Unless otherwise agreed between the Husband and Wife, the Husband shall have the right to visit Caleb and have Caleb with him, as follows: (a) The Husband may visit Caleb or have Caleb visit him at all reasonable times and places and for three (3) weeks in the summer and one (1) week in the winter, all such visits to be upon adequate notice and in deference to the child's and the Wife's existing plans; (b) Any overnight visit of Caleb with the Husband which shall last more than two consecutive nights, shall be planned with at least two weeks' advance notice to the Wife. The parties agree that Caleb shall spend approximately half of his vacation (except summer) and holiday time with each parent, and that such time shall be apportioned between the parents fairly so that each may be with Caleb on some major holidays each year and during vacation time which corresponds with each parent's vacation.

The Wife shall make every reasonable effort to facilitate the Husband's exercise of the foregoing rights; she will arrange to have Caleb ready on time for all visits and all social or other engagements made by her for the child; she shall take into account the Husband's visitation rights so that there shall be no conflict.

If the Husband is unable for any reason to exercise any of the visitation rights granted herein, he shall give to the Wife one week's notice, unless other circumstances are such that he is unable to do so. The failure of the Husband at any time to exercise the rights of visitation granted hereunder shall not constitute a waiver of these rights of visitation.

This clause in the agreement says that both of your parents agree to meet and talk about what is happening with you in school, with your health, and your growth and progress:

The Wife shall regularly inform the Husband of the progress and development of the child. The Wife shall promptly furnish the Husband whatever results and information are available with respect to report cards, aptitude, intelligence or psychological test, any evaluation of personality or character development concerning Caleb, and the results of any medical or dental examinations of the child.

In order to optimize the opportunity of contribution by both parents to the rearing of the child, to maximize the opportunity for Caleb to identify with both parents, and to minimize conflict in the child-to-adult rearing environment, the Husband and Wife agree that the following provisions shall govern Caleb's upbringing: (a) The Husband and Wife shall consult together (by correspondence or telephone if a personal conference is impractical) from time to time in an effort to mutually agree in regard to the welfare, education and development of the child to the end that, so far as possible, they may adopt a mutually harmonious policy in regard to his upbringing; (b) In the event that either parent feels that the school schedule should be changed or that the child should be transferred to another school, the Husband and Wife shall consult with each other and with Caleb and such change or transfer shall be made only with the consent of both the Husband and Wife. In the event the parties are unable to agree, the dispute regarding school schedule change or transfer shall be submitted for arbitration pursuant to the provisions in paragraph 16; (c) The Husband and Wife shall consult with each other and with Caleb regarding Caleb's participation in religious activities; (d) Ongoing medical treatment for Caleb of more than one month's duration (except psychotherapy and orthodontia) is to be planned and implemented only with the consent of both the Husband and Wife, except in emergencies; (e) The avenues of communication between both parents and the child shall be kept open at all times, and both the Husband and Wife shall have access to Caleb in person or otherwise, and Caleb to both parents for purposes of counseling, aiding, confiding and discussing any problems or concerns confronting the child or successes and awards achieved, during regular visitation periods, and during urgent, unusual, special or emergency situations.

The following clause has nothing to do with you. It is for your parents to worry about, not you:

If either the Husband or the Wife willfully or materially breaches this agreement as determined by the arbitrators or the court and the non-breaching party is required to engage counsel to enforce this agreement, the breaching party shall be required to pay the counsel fees of the non-breaching party, as determined by the arbitrators or a court of competent jurisdiction.

On a vacation, either of your parents can take you anywhere they want to in the United States. To take you out of the country they need permission from the other parent:

Both the Husband and Wife shall have the right to remove Caleb from the Commonwealth of Massachusetts during periods when Caleb is in their custody and control, during vacation or visitation periods, except that neither party shall remove the child from the continental United States without prior consent of the other party. This expense shall be borne by the parent exercising this right.

Except as otherwise provided herein, extended periods of travel (more than thirty days) of one parent with Caleb which interferes in any way with the right and opportunity of the other parent to see, take, or communicate with the child, shall be only by agreement.

This next section is easy to read and perfectly understandable, but for our own quick survey we asked four kids if their parents went by this rule and amazingly enough, all four of them answered no, that they didn't stand by this clause. That's pretty sad.

Husband and Wife agree that neither will criticize or demean the other in front of Caleb, but will at all times attempt to foster respect, love, and admiration for the other.

In the event of the child's serious illness, the first party to learn of such illness shall notify the other, or his or her designee, immediately.

Each of the parties shall keep the other informed at all times of the whereabouts of the child, if requested.

## Future Custody

This section is self-explanatory.

On the death or incapacity of the Wife, or if for any reason she no longer desires to have custody of Caleb, then the Husband shall have sole custody of the child.

## Support for the Minor Child

This section sets the amount of money that your father pays to your mother to support you. It also says that your father will be paying this support to your mother for you through your high school years.

The Husband shall pay to the Wife for support of the minor child, Four Hundred ($400.00) Dollars per month during every month in which the child is enrolled in private school or any like educational or enrichment program which shall require fees or tuition. If the child is not enrolled in any such school/program, the child support payment may be reduced to Two Hundred ($200.00) Dollars per month. These sums may be adjusted upward, and, having been adjusted upward, may then be adjusted downward, *but shall at no time be below $200.00/month.* Said adjustments shall be made in the following manner: There shall be an amount increase or decrease in the child support payment by an amount proportionate and corresponding to the percentage of increase or decrease, if any, in the Husband's gross income as it existed on April 1, 1977. Calculations shall be made annually as of April 1 of each year, and if, according to the Husband's gross income, there is an additional or lesser sums so payable, each sum shall be computed retroactively to the next previous January 1 and added to or subtracted from the monthly payments due from the Husband.

It is the intent of the parties that the child support payment shall cover the full cost of education and afterschool care for the child. The amount of child support shall thus never be less than the actual cost of such care to the Wife. Child support shall cease when the child becomes eighteen years of age or is graduated from high school, whichever occurs later.

## College Education for the Child

Your father will pay for your college education, but the agreement says nothing about further education, like graduate school:

Both parties recognize the desirability of providing Caleb with education beyond the high school level to the extent that his intellectual and emotional capacities will permit. If Caleb should decide to attend college or other professional school or training program, the Husband will pay or provide for the expenses thereof, including tuition, room and board, in a dormitory or equivalent, books and laboratory fees, and round-trip air or other reasonable transportation to and from school, all to be completed within the five years next following the child's graduation from high school. There shall be no obligation for either the Husband or Wife to provide for education on the graduate school level.

If the child, while attending school lives with the Wife, she shall be entitled to be compensated at a reasonable rate for room and board out of the educational allotment.

## Tax Consequences

Forget about this. It has nothing to do with you.

The Husband shall be entitled to claim the child as a dependent for Federal and State income tax purposes.

## Medical Insurance for Wife and Child

This part explains who pays for your medical and dental bills:

The Husband agrees to maintain a family policy of health and hospitalization coverage at least equal to his present health coverage policy in full force and effect until Caleb reaches his nineteenth birthday. By so doing, he agrees to provide health coverage for the Wife as long as he is married to the Wife or both parties are single, and as long as the Husband can do so at no extra cost to himself. The Husband's present health insurance policy is a Blue Cross/Blue Shield policy commonly known as Master Medical.

The Wife shall pay her own and Caleb's medical and dental bills and shall be entitled to receive the reimbursement of 50% of all expenses after the first .One Hundred ($100.00) Dollars of deductible/uninsured expenses is subcontracted.

It is anticipated by the parties that the child will require ortho-
dontic treatment. The cost of any orthodontia shall be shared
equally by the parties, except that if the Wife has earned income
as defined in paragraph 11, above, of more than Six Thousand
($6,000.00) Dollars per year at the time of such treatment, then
the costs of same shall be shared in whatever proportion the
parties may agree.

You have just read about the different agreements; the ones printed
above are in reference to the child. The child custody sections explain
when Caleb can see his dad. The agreement states the Caleb can see
his father three weeks in the summer, one week in the winter, and if
the boy is to stay more than one night at a time at his father's house,
it is to be planned two weeks in advance. Also, he will spend half of
every vacation with each parent. This is a very small amount of time
with his father compared to the amount of time the mother gets to see
her son. We think kids should see their parents at least enough to
keep a relationship going with each other.

The separation agreement also states that Caleb's father would pay
for Caleb to go to college. This is important for a kid to have in
writing. They do not have, however, a written agreement for who
would pay for any graduate school plans. The parents may feel that
graduate school is unimportant.

The medical aspect of the agreement says that the mother must pay
for all of Caleb's and her own dentist and doctor's bills. This is not
such a bad thing as long as her alimony or child support will cover
that.

This agreement pulls together all that should be included in a
separation and helps to avoid lots of confusion in the long run.

You may want to have a say in the separation agreement when it is
first being written. If you do, go to your parents. Don't wait for them to
come to you, because most parents don't usually go to their children
about this. There are two reasons why this is so:

1. It really puts kids in a difficult position and they may feel caught
   right in the middle.

2. Kids seem to get forgotten and lost in the fight, and parents don't usually think to ask.

The idea of having kids have a say in the separation agreement is pretty new to people and it might surprise your parents when you bring it up. Here are three tips that might make going to your parents a little easier:

1. Try not to be afraid of hurting their feelings. Be nice about it, but you've got to think of yourself and your feelings too.
2. Don't beat around the bush. This may make your parents think you're making more out of it than you need to.
3. Try to be reasonable. If you're angry about something, that's okay, but don't throw your anger at your parents right now. Be calm and direct, and get your point across.

Sometime after the agreement is written, you may feel that there is something wrong with it. In this case, your parents are definitely the first people to go to. Go right to them and tell them straight out that you would like something changed. Give your reasons and be honest.

After you talk to your parents, they may still refuse to do anything. In this case there isn't really much you can do. You could try and get in touch with the judge handling the case and ask him or her to do something about it, but they usually don't listen to kids if they are under the teenage level.

Kathy Kazanjian, a senior at Lexington High School, gave us all some good advice:

You should read the divorce agreement. You should make sure you have a place to live and money to support you. There should be something that says what happens when you turn eighteen, so your parents don't kick you out then and so that there may be money when you want to go to college. This should be in writing so that all of a sudden you're not left in the dark. Read the agreement and tell your parents that you want your concerns dealt with there in writing.

Chapter **5**

# *The Legal Issues*

Divorce and separation are complicated events. They are both emotional issues and legal issues. While it is important for us to take care of our emotional health, it is also important for us to be aware of what's happening with the legal issues.

Legal issues in divorce involve lawyers, money arrangements, and custody decisions. They can arise when both parents want the same thing in the divorce settlement, like the car, the dishwasher, or even you.

Your role in the legal issues surrounding divorce will vary depending on how much you understand and how much you feel is important to you personally. Unfortunately, your parents might not want to talk to you about the legal stuff, because they probably don't think you will understand what they're talking about, or they think that it would not be good for you to get involved. If you want to know what's going on legally in your parents' divorce, you probably *are* old enough to talk with your parents and ask them about the legal issues.

To help you understand the many legal issues of divorce, we have made a dictionary of the many terms used in legal settlements of divorce. The terms are listed in alphabetical order, rather than in the order in which they happen. If you are involved in the legal aspects, and you hear a word you don't understand, look it up.

Legal issues can really confuse kids in the divorce. Even if the issues look complicated or too big to understand, it's important for a kid to be aware of exactly what's happening in the parents' divorce. Issues are being decided which affect you, and you should make sure you have a say in how they are decided. If you sit back and let it all get figured out without you, you may regret the situation in the future.

## Alimony

Alimony is a payment, usually paid by the man to the woman. It is used for the wife to live on after the divorce. Alimony payments do not stop until one of the parents die or the one receiving alimony payments gets remarried. If it's a large amount of money, it may be used for child support. If it's not much money, it may not do much good because the woman has to pay taxes on it.

If somebody has been married for a long time, they may want to get more alimony than child support because the payments for child support stop when the child gets to be 18 or leaves school, whereas alimony stops only when either of the people die or the one receiving payment remarries. Alimony arrangements are decided by who has the money—who works and who doesn't.

## Child Support

Child support is the money that is paid specifically for the support of the kids after divorce. It is usually paid by whoever doesn't have custody of the child and goes for all the child's expenses and needs, such as clothing, food, toys, shoes, and bills.

Usually the parents have an arrangement where the mother has custody, so the father pays child support. If the father pays child support that money is not considered "income" for the mother, so there are no taxes paid on it by the mother. The money is the child's. Since it is not considered a deduction from the father's income, he still has to pay taxes on it. The payments usually go until the child is 18 or out of school, and in no way can the mother stop payments, because it's a kid's legal right to receive the benefit of the money.

The court decides how much child support is paid by looking at the income of the person who has to pay it. The judge decides how much money has to be paid at what regular interval of time; if it's not paid, it's a legal violation and can be brought to the courts. The amount of child support depends on how many kids there are and what the expenses are going to be.

Judge Edward Ginsburg of the Middlesex Probate and Family Court in Cambridge said that if child support isn't paid, the parent who is supposed to pay it may be brought before the judge and has to explain why he or she didn't pay it. If he or she has the money, he or she may be sent to jail. If he or she doesn't have it, other arrangements must be made.

The judge told us about one man who he sent to jail for not paying child support. "He wanted to tell his children that their mother sent him to jail for Mother's Day," Ginsburg said. The man had not paid the support for three months.

## Custody

Child custody involves deciding which parent or parents have legal responsibility for the decisions that affect the child, as well as physical responsibility for taking care of the child's basic needs, such as housing, food, and schooling.

We spoke with Gerry Weinstein of the Cambridge Divorce and Mediation Center. He told us about the history of child custody. Until the early 1900's, children were considered property, and, if divorce happened, the kids automatically went with their father as his property. In the early part of this century, up until the 1960's, children were generally awarded to the mother, because judges assumed that a mother made the best parent. More recently, however, people have been thinking that it's best for the children to have two parents care for them, even if the parents are divorced. Joint custody situations have become more popular and are now quite common.

There are three basic types of custody arrangements:

1. Single-parent custody
2. Joint custody
3. Third-party custody

*Single-Parent Custody.* Single-parent custody is when one parent takes full responsibility for the child or children, even when sometimes the other parent is having the child live at his or her house. With single-parent custody, the child usually lives with the mother, but this pattern is changing. The legal system that decides custody is now seeing that the sex of a person doesn't matter in this situation. Now judges are more often awarding custody to the father than they had in the past.

If through divorce your parents choose single-parent custody, you will probably basically live with only one of your parents. This doesn't mean that you will never see the other parent. It just means that most of your time will be spent in the household of one of your parents and you'll see the other for shorter periods of time.

Martin told us: "After my parents were divorced I lived with my mother. I was only about five years old and the divorce was very confusing to me. I did not see my father until about a year after the divorce. My parents probably thought that this would be better for me. As I got older, I started to see my father more and more. Now I see him on long school vacations and during summer vacation. Since I am with my mother most of the time, I really, really enjoy seeing my father."

*Joint Custody.* There are different kinds of joint-custody arrangements. There is *joint legal custody,* where both parents share equally in making the decisions about their child, but the child lives basically with only one parent. There is *joint physical custody* (also called shared custody), where both parents share equally in making the decisions, and they also share responsibility for physically housing and caring for the child. There is *alternating custody,* where parents alternate having responsibility for the child. The child lives for long periods of time with one parent (like one year) and then switches to the other parent. During the time she or he lives with one parent, that parent has full decision-making responsibility for the child. *Split custody* is not actually a joint-custody arrangement, but it has some similarities with it. It is when each parent has single-parent custody of some of their children and the other parent has the rest of them. This means that siblings may be split up.

Hannah G., who has helped write this book, lives in a joint-custody system—the alternating custody type. She was eight years old when her parents got divorced. Unlike Martin's situation, she started seeing both her parents right after the divorce. At first she lived with one parent for three days and then the other parent for three days. As she got older, the time she spent with each parent grew and grew, and now she stays with her parents at two-month intervals.

Joint custody has its good points and its bad points. One of the good things is that you get to know both of your parents pretty well. If you lived with just one parent you probably would not know the other parent as well.

Sometimes joint custody is difficult because its hard to adjust to the rules and systems of one household after you have lived in the other household for two months. Hannah's parents get along together pretty well even though they have been divorced. Parents getting along together after divorce is what makes joint custody work well.

*Third-Party Custody.* The hardest and most difficult type of custody for both parent and child is third-party custody. This is when neither parent chooses or is capable of taking care of the child or children. The court appoints a guardian to take responsibility for the child, finds a relative to take responsibility for the child, or places the child through a public agency.

We know of a girl who is in a third-party custody situation. During the divorce settlements the judge felt that it would not be good to keep this girl with either parent. Custody of the girl was given to her mother's sister (her aunt). The girl lives with her aunt, but still sees her parents every now and then. This is hard emotionally and it doesn't happen too often.

If the parents agree on who shall have custody of the child, it's a very simple matter and can be easily resolved. If both or neither parent wants custody, it's a difficult issue and may take some time to work out. If both parents want custody, the judge has to find out who would be the best at taking care of the child. Sometimes, however, both parents want custody and they can agree to joint custody.

If the judge has to decide which parent to award custody to, the judge may meet with the child and find out who he or she wants to live with, especially if the child is older. If the child is younger, the court usually gives them no choice in the matter, as they couldn't really be expected to make this kind of decision.

Often when the child is given a choice, he or she will answer "I don't care" so they don't have to make a choice. Most of the time it's hard for a child to answer the question of which parent they'd prefer to live with, because usually they're afraid of one parent being mad, or making the wrong choice. Sometimes the child feels guilty, so the judge doesn't say anything directly to the parents about the child's feelings on the matter.

Judge Edward Ginsburg told us that when the parents are fighting each other for custody rights and there's a big hearing in court, "I talk to the children privately and make up my mind. I don't like to involve the kids because they shouldn't be used as part of the fight." He doesn't ask the kids which parent they want to live with. The judge said, "This is because, most of the time, the kids love both their parents." He asks the child questions to find out which parent the child is primarily attached to—which parent the child looks to for advice. He may ask them, "If something exciting happens, whom would you call first?" This lets him determine which parent the child feels closest to.

Judge Ginsburg said that custody is sometimes the most difficult part of the divorce, and, at all times, he keeps in mind what's in "the best interest of the child."

## Decree Nisi

The *decree nisi* is a divorce decree (see below) before it is finalized. The judge will grant the decree nisi and six months later it will become a formal divorce decree. While the decree nisi is in effect, the couple is still legally married.

## Divorce Decree

As you know from the chapter on separation, a separation agreement is a written agreement between husband and wife saying who gets what and when they get it. Once the parents decide to get a divorce, if they have worked out a separation agreement, it becomes the decree nisi and then the divorce decree. When the decree is settled and finalized, the divorce is settled.

## Divorce Procedure

The *divorce procedure* (which varies from state to state) happens after the grounds for divorce are clear (the following is the procedure in Massachusetts):

1. *Meet the residency requirement:* This is when you permanently consider a place (state) your home and you plan to stay in the state a while. This is to show that you did not move to a certain place just because the divorce would be easier.

2. *Find the right court:* Each county in Massachusetts has a Probate Court and the parents may get a divorce in the county one parent lives in, or the county the other parent lives in.

3. *Meet the "thirty days living apart requirement":* Parents have to live apart for thirty days or more before they can get divorced.

4. *File a complaint:* One of your parents has to file a complaint against the other before getting divorced. This is what has to be in the complaint: both parents' names and addresses, the date and place of the marriage, the names and birthdays of the children, the date and place of the last time they lived together, why one or both of them wants a divorce, who they want to get custody and pay child support, who gets alimony.

Steps five through eight are about sending the complaint through the court and to the other parent and having them agree to meet for the trial. They are too complicated for us to explain clearly.

9. *The trial:* On the date of the trial, one of the parents will bring the separation agreement and a witness to identify the people involved. The trial often starts about 10:00 A.M. The lawyers ask the parents: What is your name and address? Are you married? What is your spouse's name and address? When and where were you married? Is this document your marriage certificate? Where did you and your spouse last live together in this state? When did you and your spouse last live together? What happened on or around that date? And was your spouse cruel and abusive to you on other occasions? Describe what happened on these occasions. Were there any children born of this marriage? What are their names and ages? Do you request that you be granted custody of these children? Do you desire the following visiting privileges to be included as part of the divorce decree, if granted? Do you desire $ — — a week for yourself for alimony and/or $ — — per week for child support? Do you wish to resume your maiden name? [only to mother] *

* Questions adapted from *Massachusetts Woman's Divorce Handbook* by Isabella Jancourtz (Second edition, 1978) pp. 18, 19. Copies of this book are available from *Divorce Handbook*, P.O. Box 743, Weston, Mass. 02193 ($3.00). Used with permission.

If your parents have signed a separation agreement, then instead of asking the last three questions, your parents' lawyer will ask them if they wish the separation agreement to be included in the divorce decree.

## Grounds for Divorce

The actual divorce procedure is the whole divorce, court and all, put into one set of events. First there are eight grounds or reasons (and a person must have one of them in Massachusetts to get a divorce):

1. *Adultery:* Adultery is when one of your parents has sexual intercourse with someone other than the other parent.
2. *Impotency:* This means that one parent, usually the father, cannot have sexual intercourse.
3. *Desertion:* This is when one parent leaves the other on purpose, but is not forced to leave.
4. *Intoxication:* If one parent has a habit of drinking heavily or taking drugs.
5. *Nonsupport:* If one parent refuses to support the other after separation, when they were expected to.
6. *Sentence to prison or jail for more than five years:* If one parent is imprisoned for a long time, the other parent may file for a divorce.
7. *The irretrievable breakdown of the marriage:* The marriage has gone too far downhill to save it.
8. *Cruel and abusive treatment:* If one parent physically or emotionally hurts the other parent.

## Lawyers

Parents usually have lawyers before they even think of getting divorced, because a lawyer is needed for a lot of other things, such as suing somebody or straightening out who pays who in a car accident. If your parents don't have a lawyer, they might call a friend to suggest one. Some lawyers are not too expensive, but some are very expensive. If your parents are looking for a not-too-expensive lawyer, they might go to a legal aid clinic and get inexpensive or free help from a lawyer.

Some lawyers turn out to be good and some turn out to be bad. This could depend on your parent's personality and on the lawyer's personality, or it could just turn out to be how much the lawyer knows. Some lawyers can be very crazy. A lawyer who doesn't think about the issues of the divorce case and just thinks about the money he or she will get is not too good. If they think mostly about the case, they're probably pretty good.

Do you feel you should be able to meet your parents' lawyers? We think kids should be able to meet the lawyers, because they are protecting your parents, and if the judge orders you into a foster home, then they will have to protect your rights too.

## Name Change

Getting names changed is part of the divorce decree. It's usually in a section of the decree called "Name Change" and it's not *your* name that gets changed, it's your mother's, maybe. In the process of getting divorced, your mother might want to get her name changed back to her maiden name (the name she had before she got married in the first place). For example, let's say you and your parents' last name is Brown. When your parents get divorced, your mother can change her name back to her maiden name. So her married name is Brown, and her maiden name was Smith—she could change her name back to Smith. That doesn't mean your name changes; it usually stays your parents' married name. But, if you wanted to, you *could* change it.

## No-Fault Divorce

No-fault divorce may be part of the divorce decree. (A no-fault divorce in Massachusetts has just recently been legalized.) The ground, or written cause of the divorce, must be "Irretrievable break-down of the marriage." This means that the parents can only get a divorce under no-fault if it is obvious that the marriage is falling apart and there's no hope of saving it.

The advantage of a no-fault divorce is that it lets parents end an unsuccessful marriage without becoming enemies in court. If both parents agree to a no-fault divorce, a *dissolution agreement* is signed by both parents. The dissolution agreement is sort of like the separation agreement because they both have things in them about custody and support. It will also have in it something about the "irretrievable breakdown of the marriage" and how both parents agreed on it.

If only one parent wants the no-fault it's a different situation. This involves a lengthy wait before the court will hear the case and a twelve-month period before the divorce becomes final. The parent who wants the no-fault divorce has to file a complaint against the other parent, saying that they thought there was an "irretrievable breakdown of the marriage." At the hearing, the parent who filed the complaint must have evidence saying that the "irretrievable breakdown of the marriage" has existed since the complaint was filed.

## *Orders*

There are four legal things called "orders" that you should know about. These orders are legal ways of dealing with emergencies that may arise before the divorce is made final. Your parents and lawyers will know about them:

The *temporary custody order* is used if you fear one of your parents might try to take you far away from the other parent. Your other parent can request a temporary custody order that will protect you from being taken away.

The *temporary vacate order* is for cases where there is a dangerous situation in the household. For instance, if your father is beating you, your mother can ask the judge to have him removed from the house. This would protect you from violence.

A *temporary support order* makes sure that you have the money to live on. The judge can arrange for your father or mother to pay this support even before the divorce agreement is finished. Its purpose is to make sure you have food, clothes, and a place to live.

One law that might be useful in any divorce is called the *temporary restraining order.* Here's what the *Massachusetts Woman's Divorce Handbook* by Isabella Jancourtz says about this order:

> A TRO forbids your husband to impose any restraint on your personal liberty. If your husband is harassing you, you can call the police, show them a copy of the order, and they can make him stop. They cannot order him out of the house, however, unless he has already moved out. Of course if your husband is actually physically beating you, you can call the police station (protective custody) whether or not you have a TRO.*

This sounds hard to understand, but it protects your mother and she may need it.

One very scary thing for a kid to go through is seeing a father physically abuse a mother. This kind of abuse and violence can some-times bring about separation and divorce and should never be allowed to continue. If your father is beating your mother, the court may not allow him to come visit you in your mother's home. This is to make sure that any kind of violence or abuse doesn't continue to take place.

## Probate Services

Probate services are services provided by the court that help the judge in making a decision about what the best custody arrangement would be for a particular family. They include family service agencies, which may investigate the parents, and counselors or psychiatric spe-cialists who may talk to the kids. Their recommendations are given to the judges before the decision is reached.

---

* Second edition, 1978, p. 7. See previous note.

## *MEDIATION*

Mediation is a new aspect of many divorces. It is an out-of-court agreement that is worked out between husband and wife with a trained mediator. Both the man and woman are present at the mediation meetings and are encouraged to express their needs, wants, and financial needs. The needs of the kids involved are also discussed. Mediation can only happen when both parents are willing to go through with it. For mediation to be successful, both people must cooperate.

There are several divorce mediation centers around the country. We spoke to people at the Cambridge Divorce Resource and Mediation Center in Cambridge, Massachusetts. The advantages of mediation are:

1. Parents are active participants in drawing up the divorce agreement.
2. Communication between the divorcing husband and wife may be improved.
3. The divorcing couple will get professional feedback about their agreement.
4. The divorcing couple may feel increased competence and effectiveness in reaching their settlement.
5. The couple will have access to other facilities and services of the divorce center.
6. There will be a substantial reduction in legal fees when compared to the cost of having two separate lawyers negotiating the settlement.
7. A workable and creative solution to problems of custody and visitation may be reached with expert, professional guidance.

## *POOR PEOPLE AND DIVORCE*

Several years ago, many people could not get divorced because they couldn't afford the various charges and fees needed to get a divorce. Usually, one parent would just walk out, sometimes forever. Because they didn't have a legal divorce, parents couldn't get remarried. This caused many problems for the parents and the children. Later, the government provided legal aid which allowed most people that wanted divorces to get them free. This caused a problem, because many lawyers were spending all their time on divorces and didn't have much time for other cases.

Today, some people still get legal aid, but not as many. This is because eligibility for legal aid is dependent on how much you make. There are more than a hundred legal aid offices in Massachusetts alone, many of them in the Boston area. Aaron Marcu, a legal aid worker at Harvard Legal Aid Bureau told us, "Poor people can get free legal help by going to their local legal aid office."

In some cases, the father (for example) has got a good job and is fairly wealthy, while the mother doesn't have a job. When they get a divorce, the father is comparatively rich and the mother comparatively poor. The alimony and child support the mother might get may not be enough to keep her off welfare, though some people definitely need the welfare money to pay for daycare for their kids while they work.

If, for example, a father makes very little money and used legal aid to get a divorce, he would pay about ten or twenty dollars (depending on exactly how much he makes) to the AFDC (Aid to Families with Dependent Children). This is a program funded by the federal government which subsidizes low income families and entitles them to certain services. It is a part of the Social Security Act and is meant to break people out of the cycle of poverty. AFDC would give something like 150 dollars to the mother and child. This aid, however, is often one of the things that politicians cut when they are tightening the budget. When it is cut, it's the children who lose out.

Another major issue with divorce among poor people is the issue of desertion. This can take place when, for various reasons, one parent just gets up and leaves and doesn't let the family know where they are. This is usually the father, and he may leave the family without a source of income. Desertion is a really difficult thing to deal with because you may feel abandoned and unloved by the deserting parent. An eleven-year-old girl we talked with told us: "My father deserted our family when I was eight and we haven't seen him. Sometimes he sends a little money, but we're basically on our own. If I saw him now I'm not sure what I'd do. Part of me would run and kiss him and part of me would punch him in the face."

Another thing that makes divorce different for poor families has to do with the fact that people don't have the money or the time to really pursue problems with the divorce settlement. If the parent who's supposed to pay alimony or child support doesn't pay it, the next step is to take them to court, and that takes money and time. Many poor people will not be able to afford to pursue the issue, and therefore they just let the settlement go.

From looking at many of the movies about divorce, like *Kramer vs. Kramer,* you'd think all families that get divorced live in condominiums in New York and both parents make $30,000 a year. This is not true. The issues for poor people that come up when they divorce are often the same as for people who are rich, but the lack of money and the economic pressures make divorce a lot more difficult for them.

Chapter **6**

# Getting Help from Counseling

Many people get the impression that counseling is only for people who are mentally ill or emotionally disturbed.

This is not so.

Though people who are mentally disturbed do go for counseling, so do other people. Counseling is a way to get help outside of the family and away from friends. People who are not mentally disturbed go for counseling to find a way to help themselves with personal or people-related problems.

Some people feel that going to therapy solves all their problems and cures everything. People sometimes feel dependent on their counselor and see them frequently. They might see them as much as once a day or several times a week.

There are several different types of counseling. One type of counseling involves going alone and discussing problems you wouldn't discuss with your family or friends. Working "one-on-one" is a good way to work with a counselor/psychiatrist on your personal problems and things that are troubling you. Your psychiatrist/counselor can help you focus on what the problem is and help you to help yourself. Going "one-on-one" is a good way to focus on specific issues and try to see what could help.

Another kind of counseling is peer counseling. Peer counseling is working with a group of about eight or nine people your own age who have similar problems. Peer counseling may also be less embarrassing than going one-on-one. Being with other people who also have problems similar to yours may make you feel more comfortable. This type of counseling is done in many age groups and it's a good way to learn to understand people and get different kinds of advice.

As you come to know more people in peer counseling, you might find that a lot of people have very similar problems and can give you a lot of support when things get difficult. Peer counseling can also be a good way to get to know different people.

---

## THE LEXINGTON HIGH SCHOOL DIVORCE GROUP

The Lexington High divorce group is a group of kids 16 and 17 who go to Lexington High School. They help other kids work out their problems concerning divorce. "It's not a group where you go in and cry on everybody's shoulder. We go out and inform kids and speak with parents and explain that we have rights, too," they told us.

The group meets once a week over lunch and talks about what they think has been going on. About 30 percent of the kids in the school are from divorced families, but not nearly that amount work with the group.

Six of the girls came to our school to talk to us about divorce: Andrea Brown, who is 17; Kathy Kazanjian who is also 17 and a senior at Lexington High, whose parents have been living apart for 4½ years but are not legally separated or divorced; Kathy Rand, 17, who lives with her mother; Kathy and Gabrielle Reem and Sharon Maloney, all 17.

This is the group's third year. The adult leader is a divorced father. He wanted a group for kids to get together and talk about their problems. They've been on radio shows, panels, debated judges and lawyers and talked with kids and parents.

"Boys don't like to open up," they told us. There are boys in the group, but they're not very active. Boys deal with divorce differently than girls. One girl told about how upset she was when her parents told them (her brother and her) about the separation, but her brother reacted nonchalantly. "I was really upset when my parents told us but my brother was like 'alright, okay, I understand,'" she said. "But when my Dad got his new apartment and invited us over to see it, my brother, I guess, was really upset and he really didn't want to go over and see it." Boys at 17 are like, "we can hack everything" and act like nothing bothers them. One girl in the group talked about the isolation she felt when her parents separated: "I felt alone, and I had no one to talk to about my feelings." She then joined the group and found other kids who had the same problems.

They also told us: "You should read the divorce agreement so you can make sure that you'll have a place to live and money to support you. There should be something that says what will happen when you turn 18 so you don't get kicked out then. That there will be money if you want to go to college, and in writing, so that all of the sudden you're not left in the dark. Read it and tell your parents you want something in there about college in writing."

The teenagers felt that it's a real effort for both parents to talk to each other after the divorce. "I was telling my mother how good it was that they were talking, and she said it takes effort," one told us. "When your parents have different beliefs it's tough. I go to my father's and I have to put on one face, then I have to go back home again and readjust."

One of the things the Lexington Group found out is that if your parents are divorced, you grow up a lot faster. In a two-parent household, if there's a problem with money the parents talk it over, but in a single parent home, the parent is more likely to come to you and say, "Hey, this is what's going on."

The Lexington High Divorce Group seems like a really good and well-organized group of kids who work hard to solve problems.

---

Another type of counseling is family counseling, which is going to a counselor with your whole family. Families go to work on problems affecting the whole family, whether it's about divorce or something else. If one of the kids in the family is violent and is having trouble living with the rest of the family, then that might be a reason to go to a family counselor. Family counseling is a type of therapy that can help the family learn to live together in a better way and maybe bring everyone a little closer.

There are several ways to go about finding the type of counseling you want and a good counselor. One very simple way is to go through your telephone book and find one. In the yellow pages you may find counselors and therapists listed under "Psychotherapists," "Psychol-

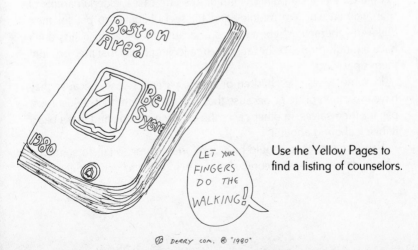

Use the Yellow Pages to find a listing of counselors.

ogists," and "Social Workers." There are centers and clinics where you can get inexpensive or maybe free counseling, such as the Cambridgeport Problem Center, Tri City Mental Health Center, the Boston Counseling Center, and Project Place (a hot line in our area).

Another way to find a counselor is to contact your doctor, who might have some good suggestions. Friends may also have helpful suggestions for counselors that might be good for the family, or just you. You really have to choose whatever way you feel most comfortable and do it. If you don't happen to like the counselor you're with, then maybe explain the reasons why you don't feel too good about what you're doing and change to another one.

You may not feel too comfortable with your counselor when you start going. The feeling may be rather insecure and touchy. A first impression may be that the counselor is trying to find out all your deepest, darkest secrets. But if you give it time, maybe it will smooth out.

People have different views on who in their family should pay the price of counseling. It can be very expensive, but for many people. it's worth it. The price of counseling can cost as much as $100 an hour, or it can be free at some places, such as Project Place in Boston.

Some parents feel that they should pay for their children's therapy with no resistance. Others feel embarrassed and tell their children that therapy is only for emotionally disturbed people and that it's a bad experience. We do not think it's bad to go to therapy, but a lot of people do feel it's a pointless thing. In some cases, elderly parents of men/women who are middle-aged still feel obligated to pay for their children's therapy. Maybe this is so because they feel their kids don't have enough money or because they're feeling guilty that they brought them up wrong.

In some cases, the children of elderly parents refuse, because they have too much pride or because they feel it's something they just must pay for themselves. In other cases the children accept, and that's okay, if they feel good about it.

Family counseling should be a comfortable time to talk to someone who understands—someone who can help you *and* your family.

Chad Dobson, a child psychologist in Cambridge, talked to us about kids and counseling. He mentioned that some kids are sometimes open and excited when they come to him for counseling, while others are timid and resistant. Kids sometimes identify him as the divorcing or abusing parent because of his beard, which may be similar in appearance to the kid's father.

"Many kids live in a mystery world of some sort," Dobson told us. This may be you. You might have a hard time saying your thoughts; we know many kids who do.

Lots of kids think that counseling is only for "baddies." Some of us once thought that too. But counseling is really for people who want it or think they need it. One boy in our class did not want counseling because he did not think he needed it. He knew what was going on and his brother was too young to know what was going on.

We think that the majority of kids who get asked to go to counseling say they don't want to go to counseling, because when kids hear grown-ups talking about people who go to counseling, they think that there is something terribly wrong with those people.

We think that some kids feel embarrassed or shy about talking to a grown-up about problems. If this is how you feel, it's ridiculous. It just shows you aren't mentally mature enough to talk to adults.

We're also sure that most kids don't want to talk about wanting counseling to their parents.

People sometimes (even a teacher) will influence kids into thinking that counseling is for "baddies" by saying things. Lots of parents don't take into consideration that the kids want counseling. If you want counseling or think you need counseling, say so.

We've talked to one kid in our school and he said that his parents' separation affected him oddly. It made him sleepy. He went to his doctor's office to see if the iron in his blood was normal. It was normal. A few weeks later he went to family counseling. He went once a week for about fifteen weeks. Gradually he felt less and less tired. He doesn't know why it affected him so weirdly. Maybe because he was depressed or mad.

We asked him some more questions about how he feels about

family counseling. He said it was a good experience for him and probably his brothers and parents, too. He said counseling can help you if you believe in it. If you don't believe in it, it can't help you. He told us that you come into a counselor's office and start talking and just keep talking about what can help you to cope with the separation and the soon-to-come divorce.

"Do the surroundings make you nervous?" we asked. "No, it's just like any other office you've been in."

"When can you talk?" "Whenever you want, but you cannot interrupt anyone else when they're talking."

"Do you like counseling?" "Yes, it's alright. At least it helped me a little."

"Do you trust your counselor?" "Yes, if you said something you don't want your parents to know about, she won't tell them."

We also talked to some teenaged girls about their experiences with counseling. One girl said, "I went to a psychiatrist because I got really messed up by the divorce. I was just not doing well in any way. My mother said to me, 'Would you want to see a counselor? Some can help work some things out,' so I went and it helped me tremendously."

She continued, "What happens depends on who you have for your psychologist. My therapist is very relaxed, it's not an office and I don't lie down on a couch. I come to her house, and we sit down in a room and she's got some chairs and pillows there. We just sit and talk. She helps me figure things out I can't understand. I can say anything I want, and do anything I want, and I don't feel inhibited. She's just helped me and taught me a lot. Our family goes once a month when a lot of things get out of hand. Sometimes you need someone who's impartial, and it helps a lot. It's really good because it's a compromise, because it's not like your mother is getting her way or you're getting your way. This way, at home, I have a lot more freedom, my mother has freedom. Things go a lot smoother. In the counseling you can yell, cry, scream—whatever it takes to get out what's bothering you, so things can get straightened out."

It's hard to decide about what makes a good or bad counselor. It really depends on who you and your parents prefer. You might have different views on different counselors. Maybe, if you don't at first agree with the counselor your parents have chosen, you could try him/her and see if he/she can help you.

You can tell if a counselor is bad for you by what *you* feel. One sort of person you may not like is the type that talks too much and gives all the advice, and says that all the things you feel are wrong. This kind of person gives you no time to say your feelings and find your real thoughts.

The sort of counselor we like is the kind who listens to you, talks with you, and gives advice as well.

It probably makes a difference also, what kind of room you're in for the counseling. If the room is very formal and stiff looking you may feel pressured and have a hard time talking. If the room is informal

---

## *THINGS TO KEEP IN MIND WHEN YOU SEE A COUNSELOR*

Don't believe everything they say as if it were absolutely true for you.

Don't let him or her tell you your personal feelings aren't valid.

Don't let yourself feel inferior to the counselor.

Make sure your counselor knows about every little detail having to do with the situation even though it might seem boring.

Don't let your counselor jump to conclusions if he or she doesn't know all the details.

Don't let your counselor put the blame on only one parent.

A good counselor wouldn't recommend that a couple stay together if that's not what they really want.

Don't let your counselor tell you you're ready to stop counseling if you don't think you're ready.

and comfortable you may feel less pressured and it would probably be easier to talk.

Some people rate good or bad counselors by their sex. Some think male counselors are best, some female. People think this way because they may be male or female and find it easier to talk to someone of a different or the same sex.

If you are going to a counselor sometimes, stop and think: "Is this counseling doing me any good? Am I any more knowledgeable about my parents' divorce? Do I know more than I did? Is it really helping me?" Maybe it is, and maybe it isn't.

## How Counseling Could Help You

Family counseling is a helpful way to sort out your problems. It can help you to find out your brother's, sister's, and parents' thoughts on the divorce. If you have counseling before the divorce it will help you to get through it. If you have counseling after the divorce it will help you to realize what has happened and how to deal with it.

Larry Hill, a marriage counselor and minister, told us, "About 30 percent of the people I talk to stay together" as a result of the counseling. A counselor can point out things that you and your parents aren't aware of. Plus the counselor can give support—support that will help you to do something that you are afraid to do otherwise, like crying

Larry Hill.

and being angry or telling your parents what you feel. All these things you might not be able to do without someone's strong support.

Mindy Sobota, a girl from our school, is seven years old. She talked to us and had some interesting points. "I think," she said, "the reason my parents fought is because they didn't like living together anymore, I don't think it was my fault."

Kids should help brothers and sisters with their problems. A girl in our class acted as a "substitute mother to her sisters." If you are an only child, discuss your problems and feelings with your parents. Sometimes you can't do these things, and that's what counselors are for.

Counseling will help your parents in much the same way as it will help you, though your feelings on the subject probably will never be the same. Counselors can help you, your brothers, and sisters to understand about divorce and how other people (children) have dealt with their own divorces. Those children's experiences might help you.

Chapter **7**

# The First Legal Day of Divorce

While you might have known for a while that your parents were going to divorce, when a divorce actually happens it can hit you hard. The first legal day of divorce, when your parents are considered no longer legally married, is when you really confront your feelings about the whole issue.

Different people find they have different feelings and thoughts about their parents' divorce. A lot of people feel resentment about the divorce, but through the process of writing this book, we've seen this kind of feeling more in younger kids than in older kids.

A twelve-year-old girl talked about her divorce experience when she was seven years old:

> At first I got mad at my mother. I felt like saying, "I'm not going to talk to you ever again." I felt like they weren't thinking of me and my brother and sisters, and that was selfish. They should stay together for me.

The anger and resentment of divorce might start to make you very upset.

A twelve-year-old boy told us about his reaction when his parents divorced when he was nine. "When my mother told me, I cried."

Three girls in our class wrote their feelings on their divorce situations and their feelings on divorce in general. Two of their parents are legally divorced and the other girl's parents are just separated:

> I am thirteen and when I was twelve my parents were legally divorced. When I was eleven my mother told me that she and my father were going to get divorced. Deep down inside me, I thought it was for the best, but on the surface, I thought they might be making a big mistake and that they could work out their problems. I also felt that there was a chance they would eventually get back together. Through the previous eleven years, they had been separated twice so the thought of them staying together still lingered in my mind, for a while.

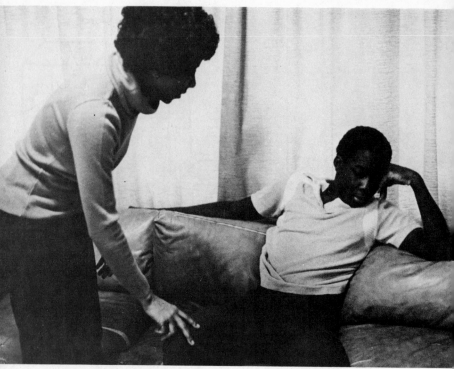

The first day of divorce.

It is very hard for me to remember what went on around the time they signed the legal papers saying they weren't married anymore, though it was only one year ago. I can remember only one thing: asking my mother approximately one week after it was over exactly what day it happened so I could put it on my calendar. It was a very trying and confusing time for me and I think that I have mentally blocked out all of it.

A lot of parents don't tell their kids in advance about the exact day of divorce for one reason or another. Do we have a right to know the date of our parents divorce in advance?

I think one has every right in the world to know as far as fairness goes.

Do we want to know? I think it might be easier if you don't have to go to sleep thinking that tomorrow is the last day of your parents' marriage. But I know I wouldn't want to be kept in the dark.

I was just 3½ years old when my parents separated. Three years later they got divorced. Many people seem surprised when they see that I'm not upset talking about my parents' divorce and how it affected me. I suppose that this is because I was so young when it happened that I don't remember it ever being any other way.

One of the few memories I have is this: A very, very sunny day, sort of the middle of the morning, maybe 10:00, and I am watching my father put all his plants in the car and drive away.

I think that basically I am happy with the way the custody arrangements are worked out. My dad, in South Carolina, I see most school vacations, and two months of the summer, and on Christmas I alternate (one Christmas with my dad, and one with my mom).

Now that I think about it, I'm glad they got divorced because their life-styles and personalities are so different. They are two totally different people.

It feels really strange going from one family to the other. It feels like going from one life to another sometimes. The friends I have in South Carolina are very different from the ones I have here in Massachusetts. I guess it's because of the way they've been brought up.

In some ways, I like living with my dad better, and in some ways, my mom. So I think that for the most part, it's evened out.

I am the 13-year-old girl whose parents aren't divorced yet. But even though they're not legally divorced, I feel that they've been divorced since the day they separated. I know that all the hostile feelings will never go away. They've been fighting ever since I can remember, although they did have a lot of good times together. I just didn't think that after all the fighting that went on they could ever work it out to get back together again. I do know that powerful emotions still linger.

The day that my parents sign the divorce papers, I don't think that I want to be kept in the dark. I trust that they will tell me before it happens because I think I should know about it. It involves my life too.

# THE DIVORCE CEREMONY

When people get married, they have a wedding ceremony. When some people get divorced, they have what is called a divorce ceremony.

Rabbi Earl Grollman of Belmont, Massachusetts has been developing this ceremony for years, and we met with him and talked about it. He answered all our questions, explained what a divorce ceremony is, and had us act out what a divorce ceremony could be like.

The divorce ceremony takes place when the husband and wife have divorced. The purpose of it is to get people to say some things to each other that are very hard to say. A divorce ceremony is a way of officially admitting that the marriage is all over. This might be hard for some parents and some kids, but it's an important thing to do.

Rabbi Grollman told us, "Divorce ceremonies take place in the sanctuary, because that's where you got married. Your children and close friends are nearby." Once the man and the woman are together in the sanctuary he says to them, "You have come together now to say goodbye to your marriage. You haven't succeeded as man and wife, but you must succeed still as mother and father of these children." People admit that their love and their marriage haven't worked out as they had hoped.

Children are given the chance to say something if they want to. Rabbi Grollman told us, "At one particular divorce ceremony, the two children were asked to speak. One said, 'I forgive you.' The other said, 'Go to Hell!' " Usually kids just get sad and don't say anything.

Rabbi Grollman also conducts many funeral services. He said, "There are as many or more tears at a divorce ceremony than most funerals."

Rabbi Earl Grollman.

It does not cost money to have a divorce ceremony. To get one, parents have to speak to someone who gives them and arrange to have it done. Rabbi Grollman feels that a divorce ceremony is a good way to say goodbye.

## Living and Visiting Arrangements

Often the most important changes that take place in your life during a divorce are in the place or places that you live and how often you will see both parents.

## Living Arrangements

There are many different types of living arrangements after a divorce; some examples follow.

*Example one.* A child lives with his or her mother and his or her father equal amounts of time. Sometimes it's three days with mom and three days with dad. Sometimes it's one week with mom and then one week with dad. Sometimes it's a month with mom and then a month with dad. Sometimes it's a year with each.

There are definitely pros and cons to this kind of situation. The

Your parents' divorce might mean new living arrangements for you—new houses, new neighborhoods, and new friends.

good things about this are that the kid gets to spend an equal amount of time with both parents and therefore gets to know them equally well. To have this situation, the parents have to be on good terms with each other and understand what their kids are going through. If they're not on good terms, there can be lots of jealousy and bad feelings; the kids often become the messenger between parents. When that happens you know that the situation is not working out. Jokingly, we think the only thing that's good about this situation is that a kid has a room at both mom's and dad's home.

*Example two.* The children live with one parent during the year and go to visit the other parent on vacation. This works out pretty well, except that the parent who only gets the kids on school vacations usually feels jealous and would like to spend more time with them and see them more often. There is one other problem with this arrangement. If the kids have to leave on every school vacation, the children never get to see their friends, which means that the kids miss out on a lot of stuff that goes on.

There are other living arrangements, such as when the kids have to live with their grandparents because their parents have to get things worked out or can't deal with the kids at that point. We can't begin to describe all the living situations, and there are plenty of unique cases. Parents usually decide the custody arrangements with each other. Sometimes they go to court when it becomes bad and the court has to decide for them.

To show how many different types of living situations there are, we took a survey of the divorced kids in the class. Here is a list of how some of us live and how we visit:

- Sophie Aikman lives with her mother in a house in Cambridge and visits her dad, who lives in the same neighborhood, once a week and for two or three weeks in the summer. She has her own room in both houses, and in her mom's house in New Hampshire, too. Her brothers and sisters go to school in the winter but live with her in the summer.
- Martin Albert lives with his mother and brother in a house in Cam-

## IF ONE PARENT DROPS OUT OF YOUR LIFE

Sometimes divorce means that you won't see a parent for a long time — even forever. This parent is often called an "absent parent." If one parent leaves when you are very young, you may not notice it very much. One boy we interviewed said, "Since I grew up without a dad, I never noticed that I was missing something." His father left when he was six months old.

Whether your parent left when you were young or old, you may have a lot of questions. If you do have unresolved feelings you are apt to feel betrayed, abandoned, maybe even unloved. Try to talk with your other parent or a close relative. If you find an explanation, you will begin to deal with the reality of the situation.

In the movie *Kramer vs. Kramer* we see an absent mother situation. Joanne decides she can't live happily with her son and husband anymore. Because she had been young when she was married, she found herself in a relationship which didn't let her do what she really wanted to do. Joanne loved her son, Billy, very much, but she didn't think she could be a good mother or wife any more, so she left.

We wonder if Billy Kramer felt something like Bernie, a fifty-four-year-old court clerk from New York, who told us about being just four years old when his father left: "I felt as if everything was my fault." He didn't have any other brothers or sisters to convince him that it really wasn't his fault. For a while, Bernie thought that he had been "bad" or something and that's why his father had gone. If Bernie had a brother or sister there it might have been easier for him.

Having a parent drop out of your life is not a good experience, but it shouldn't be ignored. It is something that the family members who remain must pull together and deal with.

bridge. He has his own room on the top floor. He goes to visit his dad in Bucks County, Pennsylvania, almost all vacations. His dad built his own house and lives in it with Martin's stepmother and four stepbrothers and two stepsisters. Martin shares a room with his stepbrother.

- Matthew Allison lives with his mom in an apartment in Cambridge, and he has his own room. He visits his dad, who lives in a brownstone in Brooklyn, New York, all school vacations and for a month in the summer. His dad's girlfriend lives there, and Matt has his own room.

- Louis Crosier lives in a two-family house in Cambridge with his mom and his dog.

- Regan Day lives in a house with her mom and stepfather and two brothers. She visits her dad in Poughkeepsie, New York, every two months.

- Hannah Gittleman lives for two months with her mother in a two-family house in Cambridge. Her brother and her mother's boyfriend live there, and sometimes her three stepsisters. When the stepsisters aren't there, she has her own room. Every two months she switches to her dad's house in Watertown where she lives with her brother and three boarders. She does a lot of visiting back and forth.

- Mike Kearney lives with his mom and lots of roommates and a dog and cat in an apartment in Cambridge, where he has his own room. He visits his dad in New Orleans on Christmas and summer vacations, where he lives with two stepbrothers, his stepmother, and a dog. He shares a room with his eldest stepbrother.

- Denise Lewis lives with her mother and cat Maggie in a house in Malden. Her dad sometimes picks her up after school and spends time with her.

- Heather Murphy and her two sisters live with their dad on Monday, Tuesday, Wednesday and every other weekend. Her dad lives in an apartment in Back Bay, Boston, with his girlfriend and a cat named Tashie. On Thursday and every other weekend the girls live with their mom in a two-family house in Medford with two kittens, a dog, and a hamster. This arrangement changes every six months.

- Jenny Perrelli and her sister go to their father's house one day and their mother's the next day. They live in Roxbury in houses right across the street from each other. In her dad's house she has her own room and in her mom's house she shares a room with her sister.

- Tom Rasmussen lives with his mom and stepfather in Cambridge. He doesn't see his father.
- Laura Spiro and her brother live in a condominium in Cambridge with their mom and three cats during the week and with their dad and four gerbils in a Boston apartment on weekends.
- Sarah Steele lives with her mom, her sister, two cats, and some boarders in a house in Cambridge. She has her own room. She visits her dad in a house in Mt. Pleasant, South Carolina on most school vacations. She has her own room there.
- Jon Tupta lives with his mom, two brothers, three cats, three fish, two doves, two hamsters, and one dog in a house in Newton Centre. He has his own room. He visits his dad in Ohio summers and lives with his dad, his dad's secretary, his brothers, and one goldfish.

## Parents Who Live Far Away

It's really hard when one of your parents lives far away. Most kids feel that it's very hard to deal with the fact that both their parents don't live close together anymore. Even when you only get to see one of your parents once a year, it might be fun to look forward to seeing them at that time. While it's always nice if your parents live close

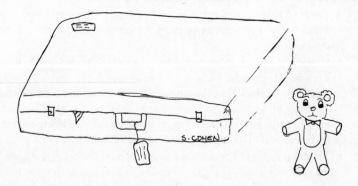

together, it might be kind of fun if one of your parents lives in Massachusetts when it's cold in the winter and you get to go to the other parent's house in Florida!

You might find it hard if one of your parents asks you if it's all right with you if they move away. We can't tell you what to do in this situation, it's really your decision. You should take into account that it's not mainly your decision. It might be a good idea if you and your parents made the decision together.

One thing that comes to mind for most kids is how they're going to get to the other parent's house. This usually depends on how far away one of your parents lives.

If one of your parents lives very far away from the other, you'll probably end up going to see them on a plane, or sometimes a train. If your parents live about fifty miles away, you'll probably end up taking a bus. You really should let your parents decide how you're going to get there, in most cases, though you should let them know how you feel.

If you're going by air you might be wondering what happens if you get on the wrong plane and you fly to China. Well, this really could never happen, so don't worry about it. Airplane people make sure it doesn't happen. When you're traveling by yourself, the stewards and stewardesses are really nice to you and can be very helpful.

There are a couple of kids in our class who have to take the plane to the other parent's house. Jon Tupta lives with his mom in Massachusetts and his dad lives in Ohio. Jon says, "Well, it really wasn't too bad going by plane, in fact it was kind of fun. The stewardesses were really nice. They showed us where to go, and where to sit, and everything. I really wasn't too scared at all, but my brothers were."

Traveling by train is another story because there's no one in our class who travels by train regularly, but we've heard that the conductors are really nice to you.

We think going by bus is one of the easiest ways to travel. If you sit by a window it can be fun to watch the scenery go by. Traveling can be scary the first time you do it, but after a couple of times you get used to it.

Visiting a parent who lives far
away can mean getting used to
buses, trains, or planes.

## *Picking Sides and Other Hazards*

Picking sides between your two divorced parents can be a problem, but you don't have to pick sides at all. Your parents know that divorce is hard on you, but again, you have to remember it's hard on them, too. Even if one of your parents seems upset, and the other seems mean at times, it's just a stage they're going through. It's better not to pick sides, because if they're going through a hard time it could turn into a harder situation for everybody.

If your parents are divorced, you might have problems going back and forth from one house to the other house. One of your parents picking you up without any notice and getting the other worried can cause problems. Someone might not pick you up when they're supposed to, making *you* worried.

Some parents ask you everything that happened when you were with the other parent. Should you tell? Everything is hard when people are divorced. There's so much that you don't understand, so much that is confusing. If parents go through such trouble, why do they ever get married? Should you pick sides? If so, whose side should you pick? We don't have the answers. Again, we suggest that you talk with someone about it, especially if you don't think you can just sit at home weekends and think. If nothing seems to work when your parents are getting divorced, just let it go along and work itself out.

How am I going to get used to going back and forth between houses? What clothes should I bring and where should I keep them? How much money can I have for an allowance? What's it going to be like with two sets of friends? Who's going to take better care of me? Should I love one parent better than the other? Who's going to answer all my questions? No one person can answer all your questions. But if you can't find anyone who can answer your questions don't worry. And remember, they're *both* still your parents.

If people seem to be extra calm about the divorce, and parents are bothering you about whether or not you're happy with the other parent, don't tell them, because they might use it in court or at home. Just say everything is okay.

Some of the worst feelings in divorce come when the kids have to go back and forth from one parent to another. Sometimes kids feel uncomfortable having a phone conversation with one parent when the other parent is in the room.

Kids' feelings about going back and forth from one parent to another often come out in hostility toward one of the parents. Going back and forth from one parent to another puts you in the position of getting used to the different worlds of your mother and your father. It's hard to describe all the feelings kids have, because each kid has a different feeling or reaction to divorce. All we can tell you about is our feelings and concerns.

## Holidays

Holidays are one of the hardest things for most kids to deal with and get adjusted to after a divorce. From our point of view, Christmas is really one of the major holidays to deal with.

It's really quite hard for you as a kid to deal with and make a decision about holidays. Holidays are much easier if your parents live close together. One student in our class said, "My parents live right around the corner, so I spend Christmas Eve with my dad and Christmas with my mom."

It's hard to make the decision about Christmas (and other holidays) if your parents live far away. This is the case of a girl in our class, Sarah Steele; her mom lives in Massachusetts and her dad lives in South Carolina. She said, "Well it really isn't that bad because I alternate holidays. So when I have Christmas with my mom, my dad sends my presents through the mail, and when I'm with my dad (since I live with my mom) I just have Christmas a little late when I get back from my dad's."

Some parents even try to get back together just for Christmas.

There's no one in our class who has a situation like this, but we've heard that it's very hard for the parents, and it makes them feel very awkward. We've also heard that for little kids between the ages of three and eight, it makes Christmas much happier for them.

Although we've mostly been talking about Christmas, there are other holidays kids have trouble with: Hanukkah, Thanksgiving, Easter, birthdays, and also summer vacations. There are so many different ways to deal with these holidays that we bet there aren't two arrangements exactly the same. In some ways we think it's best (most of the time) to let your parents decide about holidays, because then there's not so much pressure on you.

## Leading Two Different Lives

Leading two different lives when you live with one parent and then the other can be very confusing. We think that one of the ways to get used to this is feeling free with both parents. A girl in our class says that one of the things that made it easier for her to get used to going

Some parents can be very understanding.

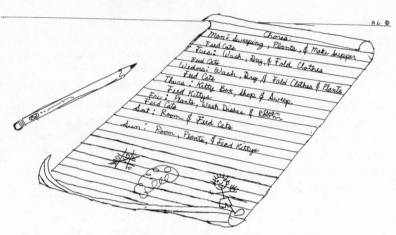

It's sometimes hard keeping track of your chores in new living situations.

When you first move into a new home, it's good to spend time in your room and get used to the new surroundings.

back and forth from one parent to another was that her mother was very understanding. Most kids do feel like they need a little help from their mother or their father.

Parents can help by:

1. Helping us understand clearly the rules in each house and not getting mad if for the first few weeks we make some mistakes.
2. For the first little while we should basically stay at home and be allowed to get used to the new surroundings. It's not a good idea to take us out everywhere when we've just found a new home.
3. It would be really helpful if parents remembered that the kids are still kids and shouldn't have a whole lot of responsibilities put on them.

Sometimes the parents are so preoccupied with what they're going through, it's hard for them to realize what their kids are going through. At these times the kids have to pull through it all by themselves.

Chapter **8**

# Weekend Santa

The weekend Santa can be a part of any divorce. If you're living with your mother and you visit your father on the weekends, he might be jealous because your mother gets to see you more than he does. While you're visiting your father, he may try to be nicer to you than your mother by buying you presents, because he is jealous. He's being a weekend Santa.

Keep in mind that there is a difference between bribery and making a kid feel better. Bribery occurs when a mother says, "Here, Johnny, if I give you a lollipop, will you stop crying?" In this example, Johnny's mom would be trying to bribe him into not crying.

Your parents might be trying to ease their guilt by buying you presents. If you don't see one of your parents, let's say your father, very much, he might give you more games, toys, and candy than your mom when you do see him. This is because he is trying to make up for the times he doesn't see you. Because you are with him for a short time, he tries to give you all the good things in just a couple of days, which your mom would give you in a few weeks. Some fathers have never spent much time with their kids and really don't know what to do with them. Because they don't want to seem like bad fathers, they fill in the time by giving treats. Other fathers really want to give their kids a lot both emotionally and materialistically and only have a few days to do it in. Your mom probably doesn't buy you as many things as your dad. Since you see her more, she probably thinks that the love and time she spends with you replaces presents. Some mothers in this situation do give you as much as the weekend Santa, but they spread it out over a lot of time so it seems like less.

Tony, a boy we know whose parents were recently divorced, has an interesting situation now with the weekend Santa. He told us that he loved his father more than his mother, because whenever he is at his father's house, there is always "Milky Way bars, Pringle potato chips, and lots of other junk food!" His father also gave him a lot of presents, like records, animals, and tickets to concerts and ball games. It seemed obvious to us that his father was buying his love, not just because of the gifts or the food, but because Tony said his father let him "get away with murder." Tony and his brothers are allowed to scream and fight constantly, stay on the phone for hours, and cop out on their household chores. This may make Tony happy for a while, but in the long run he may feel resentment toward his father.

Andrea, another girl we know, lives with her father, and her mother plays the weekend Santa. Andrea told us, "I know that my mother

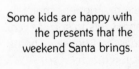
Some kids are happy with the presents that the weekend Santa brings.

makes the time we spend together very special. We do fun things like go to movies and to stores and parties and I'm glad she makes sure I have a good time. What I don't like is when she tries to outdo my dad. Once my dad gave me a pair of sneakers and I wore them to my mom's house for the weekend. My mom saw them and right away took me out and bought me a more expensive pair of sneakers. When I went back to my dad's house he took me out and bought me a pair of running shoes. Before I knew it I had five pairs of sneakers and track shoes. I liked having so much footwear, but I hated the fact that my parents were trying to prove they were better than each other by the sneakers they bought me."

There are some Santas who deal with things other than material gifts. One type we know is called the privilege Santa. This Santa gives his or her kids many privileges or lets them get away with a lot of behavior that normally wouldn't be permitted. A girl we know named Lola has a father who doesn't like to discipline the kids in any way. He thinks the kids' time with him should be "perfect," and he thinks discipline would disturb a pleasant visit. As a result, his kids can do almost anything they want. Lola's father is a privilege Santa.

Parents who don't see their children as often as their ex-spouse sometimes feel they have to make up for lost time by spending a lot of time with their kids. This parent may become what we call an overtime Santa. For instance, if you are in your room, doing something on your own, the overtime Santa may come in a million times in an hour to tell you lots of incidental things like, "I'm making dinner, now!" or "What do you think of putting celery in the salad?" or "It sure is a nice day today!" This Santa may get to be a bother. Remember, however, that overtime Santas really do mean well.

Judy, a girl we interviewed, said, "I don't see my mom as much as my dad. Whenever I'm at my mom's house she wants to spend every minute with me. It makes it hard to consider her house a home because she seems uptight and self-conscious too much."

Some kids only see a parent during a vacation. A girl we know named Joyce has a father who lives across the country. Joyce told us, "It's strange not being able to just see him whenever I please — to visit, to get away, or if there's something special going on in my life. While I am visiting him, it's always for too short a time and I want to express everything I think and feel. It's hard to fit it all into one short month." When a parent sees their child(ren) for a short time each year, he or she may have the characteristics of a weekend Santa, a privilege Santa, or an overtime Santa. Let's just call this parent the vacation Santa.

Kids have different feelings about Santas. Some kids just think, "Oh boy, I'm getting all these presents! Mom or Dad is being very nice!" Some kids might have many questions in their minds, for example, "Why does the parent I see less give me the presents and not the parent I see more?" or "Why is my parent buying me presents and doing lots of things for me?" or "Why is it that my father is giving me presents now and not before my parents got divorced?" There are many more questions than those. If you read back a bit to the first example, we will try to give you some idea of why you or somebody would feel these things.

*Not Noticing.* Some kids, especially little ones, won't notice that their parents are bribing them or giving them gifts. They are just happy with the presents they get.

*Noticing.* Some kids will notice that their parents are being weekend Santas or bribing them, but don't *care* that they are, because they are getting some great presents. They don't care why their parents are doing it.

Some kids have fun comparing their gifts from weekend Santas.

*Resentment.* Some kids may feel resentment because they don't think it's right that their parents have to bribe them. Presents won't make up for time. If a parent gives you only presents and not time, it's sort of a cop-out on their part. But a parent supporting you with an occasional present is okay.

*Guilt.* Some kids feel guilty when a parent is trying to make up for something by giving the kid presents. The kids feel guilty because their parents are spending money on them instead of buying something else. Since the kids don't really need the presents, they feel guilty because the money is going to waste.

We talked to parents about bribery, and some of them said that they think most kids are easily bribed. One parent said, "I think kids are bribed easily because bribery confuses them."

Kids are not the only ones bribed easily. Adults can also be bribed. Here's an example of a kid bribing an adult: "Mommy, if I don't bother Pete, can I have a cookie?" Bribery is easy to pull off because everybody likes to get presents.

Some parents think it's fine to be Santas. They say that the kids don't understand what is really going on and they think that their parents are being especially nice. If your parents give you gifts sometimes, that's fine. It's not fine when their gifts are substitutes for the time spent with you.

Chapter **9**

# Stepparents and Other People

Sooner or later you have to admit that your parents aren't going to go out with each other anymore. Either they're going to sit at home not seeing anyone but you or they're going to go out with someone else. The latter is probably the case.

## *Dating: What's It About?*

Dating usually happens after the divorce, but sometimes it happens after the separation. Your parents date because they want to meet new people, even though they might still be sad or angry about what has happened in their family.

Dating is about meeting new people and getting your parent's mind off things. In a lot of cases, people are trying to get divorce out of their minds. New people can help them do that.

It may hurt to imagine your mother or father out on a date. You have to understand that divorce is a very rough thing and your parents get the worst of it. It is hard to say when dating really begins. You just have to notice when he or she starts going out frequently and comes back happy.

Do you want to meet your mother's or father's date? You may not want to meet their date because you are embarrassed or afraid of them or afraid of what they're going to say about you, or what they might do to you mentally or possibly, physically. They might shower you with gifts and try to win you over from your true parent. On the other hand, they might be really nice and not do this.

Laura, a girl in our class, told us about meeting her father's girl-friends: "For some reason I like to meet my father's girlfriends. One girlfriend of his and I became very close. She told me that when she met me she was nervous and self-conscious. I never thought girlfriends or boyfriends felt that way, but it makes sense."

Dating can be confusing for both you and your parents. You may resent your parent's new girlfriend or boyfriend, or you may like them. They may have kids of their own who may have to play with or live with you for a while. Since you will have to live with the parent the court awards you to, you should always have a say in who they live with or who they marry.

Do you feel odd having one of your parents go out on a date with someone you hardly know or don't even know at all? Do you think your parents should introduce you to the person they are going out with? If you do, it is perfectly natural. If there have been several dates and you want to meet the woman or man, request to meet them or just introduce yourself. If you don't want to meet the man or woman, you should think twice about not meeting that person, even if you don't know anything about them. If you find you don't like them, tell your mother or father and hope they take your feelings into consideration.

Not knowing what is going on with dating is one of the worst things that can probably happen. How would you feel if the parent you're living with tells you that he or she is going out for a few hours with some friends and leaves you at home by yourself and doesn't come back until morning? Do you think this is fair? We bet you don't. In fact, you would probably be enraged and want to get revenge and make them feel the same way by playing hooky or damaging their property. We suggest you don't. If you wait a little while, and if your parent is really smart, he or she might realize what he or she is doing and start telling you what has been going on.

## New Relationships

If your parents start bringing someone home regularly, you have to learn to relate to them, and you also have to relate to your parents after they start talking about someone else and thinking about someone else. Relating to your mother's or father's friends after the divorce may be hard, especially if they have known your parents before the divorce.

A new person could change your relationship with your parents in many different ways. You could feel as though you were once the main part of your parent's life, but when they divorced and started going out with someone else, you might begin to feel left out. If you feel this way, you'll probably be wondering if it's okay to hate the person your parent keeps bringing home. Well, it doesn't really matter whether you hate

Laura has many thoughts about her mother's fiancé.

them or not, as long as you keep those private thoughts inside and don't show them too much on the outside.

A girl named Lucy talked about her father's girlfriend. She said, "I had a cat who was my best friend and my father's girlfriend started bringing her dog to visit. My cat soon ran away." Lucy was resentful of the woman.

Sometimes, however, things just pop out without you wanting them to, and that's why you should learn to relate to the other person. You could get to know them better by talking and asking questions about them, and then they might feel more relaxed talking with you. Try to see it from your parent's point of view; they feel a need for another companion now that they're divorced, someone other than you.

In some cases you may like the person. You may be able to see in them what your parent sees in them and like them for it. Maybe they even understand you better than your parents do.

When you talk to one parent about the other it may be embarrassing for you. Now that your parents are divorced they shouldn't worry about each other so much, so they may not ask many embarrassing questions. They should find their own friends, and you should help them by not being hostile to the friends they bring home.

Your relationship could change with your mom or dad if you feel as though either parent has more time for a girlfriend's or boyfriend's kids and a girlfriend or boyfriend than you. But this is not usually true. Your parents love you just as much as they always have and always will. Karen Kazanjian from the Lexington High School Divorce Group felt this way until she realized that her father had to give time to his friends as well as to her:

My father's thinking of getting remarried and his girlfriend lives in Acton and she has two small kids. And one of the things that I had to get used to was, we'll go out there and he'll spend Saturday mornings with them, and watch cartoons with them. I used to resent that, as he never did it with me. But he has his own life to lead now and if it's going to make him happier to be remarried, I'm not going to stop him.

How should you address or introduce your parent's girlfriend or boyfriend? A girl in our class sometimes feels like introducing her father's girlfriend as "That asshole who sleeps over once in a while." You may feel like saying that, but cover up and introduce her or him normally. Sometimes it may be embarrassing to introduce them as "my father's girlfriend" or "my mother's boyfriend." It may make you feel as though you're stating your parents' divorce out loud for everyone to hear. That can be a strange feeling, but you'll get used to it soon enough. Hannah, a girl in our class, told us about an awkward situation: "We were all at a school pot-luck dinner and my father and his girlfriend were there together. Someone asked me if they were my parents, so I said, 'This is my father and, see, my parents are divorced, so this isn't my mother.'"

Another thought that has probably been in your mind is "What if my parent gets married to this person they're seeing?" Then the divorce is final; final because they're divorced now and my mother or father has gotten married to someone else. This is one of the most difficult things to face.

It is very important to let your parent know how you feel about their "friend." Before they have decided to remarry, they will probably have the person stay the night. This could feel strange if you didn't know the person properly and your parent hadn't yet asked your advice or permission to have the person over. You might feel that your mother's boyfriend is taking over your mother's love for you or is taking over the place where your father should be—and where *you* should be.

In the movie *Kramer vs. Kramer* there is a scene which relates to what we're talking about. Ted Kramer, the father, has a woman spend the night in his apartment. Billy, Ted's son, gets out of bed in the middle of the night at the same time Ted's girlfriend is going to the bathroom—naked. When they run into each other, it is very embarrassing, and she introduces herself as "a friend of your father's." Billy's reaction is to ask her if she likes fried chicken. Then he went right to bed. He must have felt strange—like anyone would if they ran into a naked stranger in their house.

When your parent has been going out with a girlfriend or a boyfriend for some time, the friend may start taking or bringing you places. They could take you:

- on a bike ride;
- on a weekend trip;
- to work with them;
- out shopping;
- for a boat ride;
- for a walk in the country.

These events can help you get accustomed to this person, and you might have fun. You can get to know them alone, without another person there. This should be a good experience, because you should learn to relate to different situations and people, especially special people in your parents' lives.

Flying a kite is one thing you could do with a new stepparent.

## Stepparents

*Stepparent:* A stepfather or stepmother.
*Stepfather:* The husband of one's mother by a later marriage.
*Stepmother:* The wife of one's father by a later marriage.
*Stepchild:* The child of one's spouse by a former marriage.

A stepparent is someone who is married to your mother or father after one of them has been divorced or has died. A second marriage causes you to have a stepparent.

If you have a stepparent, you may not feel too close to him or her when he or she first comes into the household. If the name you call your stepparent is a big issue, then you might start calling him or her by their first name, to make sure that you don't confuse the role of mother or father with stepparent. If you make friends with a stepparent quickly, then you might start calling them "mom" or "dad." Calling a stepparent "mom" or "dad" may seem awkward or feel uncomfortable at first, but if you feel that calling them "mom" or "dad" is an okay thing for you, then call them that. If the feeling is such that you feel uneasy and awkward about calling them "mom" or "dad," and you feel like you're obligated to call them that because they would feel offended if you didn't, then try discussing it with them and get their feelings on the matter.

If you want to keep the roles of your original parent and a stepparent very clear, then you might feel most comfortable calling them by their first name or a nickname. The stepparent, male or female, is going to feel rather uneasy about how the kids from the original family feel about them and would probably like to talk about their relationship with you.

Some of us know from experience that having a stepparent is a very difficult thing. We think having a stepparent causes the kids from the original family to feel out of place and confused about what role the stepparent plays. But the kids from the original family may take very well to the stepparent, and then it isn't a problem at all. But if the situation is such that one or any of the kids dislikes the stepparent, this

Stepparents might feel awkward when they first start living with you.

can present a very difficult problem that makes it hard for the "new" family to live with each other in a good way.

A girl in our class wrote about her stepfather:

> I have a stepfather who has been living with my mother, my two older brothers and myself for the past eight years. My brothers and I found it fairly easy to have a stepfather at first because we were young when he first came to live with us. But as time went by, each of us, at different stages, found it hard to live with a stepfather. I found it hard at some points because my stepfather

and I would be talking and by accident I would slip on a word and get my sentences messed up. He then would get angry because I got the wrong message across and while I was trying to sort out what to say, he would be lecturing me on how I shouldn't get things fouled up like that. My brothers have had conflicts about decisions my stepfather would make and it usually ended in an in-depth, heavy and emotional discussion. But at one point, or another, each of us discussed the situation and tried to understand that, if he didn't like you to do that, then avoid the situation. For me, at least, it was just trying to find out where my stepfather stood in my life and I would try not to trespass into his privacy and he tries to do the same.

When a stepparent comes into a family, it's hard to maintain a decision between the original parent and the stepparent about beliefs and expectations. When a stepparent is brought into a situation in which the family has already dealt with an issue — such as whether they're going to church or not, or if the kids are allowed outside after dark — it's hard for each person to adjust to that change. Each person might have to change their expectations to meet the other person's needs. This may result in compromises on both sides or decisions made by the "new" family about particular things.

Probably a common conflict that an original parent and stepparent have is whether or not to practice religion. If one does practice religion and the other doesn't, how do you deal with it? It's something that the whole family sits down and decides. In some cases people can be very easy going about it, and it doesn't make too much difference one way or another. It really depends on the kind of family it is and how the kids have been brought up.

Being a stepparent is a very difficult task to take on when entering a marriage. Some parents don't realize the living arrangement problems involved when a stepparent is brought into the situation. Who gets to make adult decisions when the original parent is not there and the stepparent is left in charge of the kids?

A boy named Kenny talked with us about his stepfather. He said, "I get mad at my stepfather because whenever he is upset about something me or my sister do, instead of bringing it up himself, he has to get my mother to yell at us."

A stepparent left in charge over the other parent's kids faces difficulty because the kids sometimes don't respect the stepparent's opinion and feel they have no right to set down rules if they're not the parent. It's hard for both the stepparent and kids to understand the other guy's feelings and anger. It takes time for the stepparent and the kids to see each view and learn a way to work out how the kids can go by what the stepparent says. The stepparent also has to understand how the kids feel about someone else making a decision that their parent would originally make.

Some stepparents really enjoy being stepparents and fit into the "new" family very well. They feel very close to the kids of the original family and love them very much. As long as the kids from the original family take to this, it works out very well.

Other kids from the stepparent's family can be a whole lot of fun, "a real bummer," or they can bring about a very neutral situation. In some cases, the stepparent has his or her kids come to visit them during the summer, a few vacations, weekends or a variety of other arrangements — it really depends on how the living arrangement works. Sometimes the stepparent doesn't see his or her kids very often or at all (but this isn't too common).

Other kids from stepparents can live within the household with the other parent's kids all the time. If the stepparent's kids are living in the household, then it might take time for everybody to adjust to a change like this. It can be very difficult for each set of kids to relate to each other, depending on their ages.

Kids from stepparents can act more like friends than like stepbrothers or stepsisters. Some kids find their stepparent's kids to be like other kids that are there on weekends or during a few vacations and are just something that happens, and that's all there is to it.

It is common for kids to hate their stepparent's kids, and sometimes there is no way for the two sets of kids to get along. For the children of the original family, having kids that aren't related to them suddenly come into the household may seem like an intrusion on their environment. This intrusion can make the situation such that the kids from the original family resent their parents for remarrying and make it hard for the household to move at an even pace.

If the two sets of kids don't get along with each other, maybe the "new" family should get together and try to work out a way that everyone can live with one another and have respect for each other. Maybe each set of kids should keep their distance from the other and try to make the best of the living arrangement.

If it seems hard at first to relate to a stepparent and their kids, maybe time would help by giving each person space to find out where he or she stands in the new household. If time passes and things still seem difficult, then you should try talking to the person that seems to be in conflict with you; see if talking doesn't help to improve the situation.

If one of your parents remarries, they may decide to have another kid or a few more kids. These new kids would be your half brothers or half sisters. These new people in your life may cause you to feel many things. Laura said, "My mom isn't going to have more kids with her new husband but, if they did, I would be so jealous. I would feel they were taking some love away from me for that new kid."

Stepparents and other people are not necessarily bad and don't necessarily cause problems for kids. Here are two stories about kids who had good experiences with their stepparents:

When I was twelve my father brought home a new girlfriend. When I first met her I don't really remember what I thought of her. I *did* think that she was nice but I didn't think much about it at all. As time went by I got to know her and her three kids well and she got to know all my friends. When my father or anyone was upset, she would be really helpful.

Once I was upset about boys and she made everything seem so clear. I also got to be good friends with her oldest daughter and even after she and my father broke up we did things together. Her youngest son once called me up to ask advice and to this day it is our secret. So girlfriends and fathers can be a good thing. I have proof now. Now that they have broken up I am very picky about who my father sees. I still see his old girlfriend and we do things like go to the beach. I am glad my father went out with her because I have a great friend as a result.

Less than a year ago my mother started going out with this guy named Allen. I always thought he was a nice guy. One night when he was over (they were practically living together), I asked my mom if I could move the stereo into the living room. She said, "No, you can't. I may as well tell you now..." She called my brother Daniel in and she told us of their plans to be married. They were to move their bedroom into the living room. That's why I couldn't move the stereo in there.

I was hesitant about this marriage. It surprised me so much that I didn't know what else to do but dislike the idea. I talked to my friends about how they had only known each other for a while. I convinced myself their marriage wouldn't last more than a year. I was probably upset because of such a surprising decision. I changed my mind quickly.

After I got used to the idea of their marriage, I began to like the idea more and more. Maybe because the shock wore off. Whenever I had a problem, Allen would always help, sometimes better than anyone else. We found similar interests, like music, skiing, and sailing.

Now I am looking forward to their wedding in another month. Allen can figure out family problems better than anyone because he is new to the situation. Best of all, Allen and my father get along well.

In my mom and Allen's wedding ceremony they have decided to include a part which basically says that Allen is not only accepting my mother as his wife, but Daniel and I as his stepkids. I am looking forward to being related to him and his family.

A divorce is a situation that changes your life. You experience new feelings, new relationships, and you enter new kinds of families. It is important for all kids from divorced families to be open to these changes and see in them the possibility of new growth and new fun. Only by allowing us to be open to our new lives will we begin to get over some of our bad feelings and start a healing process.

## *LOVING YOUR GAY PARENT*

Most people go on dates with people of the other sex. Your mother may see some men other than your father who she just got divorced from; your father may see other women. Some parents realize that they are interested in forming relationships with people of their own sex. Your mother may start dating other women; your father may date other men. This means that they have homosexual, or *gay,* feelings.

We looked in Webster's Dictionary and found the meanings of several words that have homosexual implications:

- *Homosexuality:* Sexual desire for others of one's own sex.
- *Lesbian:* A female homosexual.
- *Gay:* Homosexual, slang.
- *Fag:* A male homosexual, slang.

We asked several kids what they thought these words meant:

- *Lesbian:* A woman who would rather have a "husband and wife" type of relationship with another woman.
- *Gay:* A word used to put homosexual people in a group.
- *Fag:* A man who would rather have a "husband and wife" type relationship with another man.

Being gay is a form of relationship. It in no way limits a parent's ability to bring up a child. Society has put down the gay parent (and gay people in general) in obvious ways. When you think of a gay man, the first thing that comes to mind is the stereotype of a "fag"—tight yellow or pink pants, feminine shirt, and stuff like that. Being gay is love for the same sex, the same kind of love two people have when they want to marry. Some gay people dress in outrageous ways, but most gay people don't. Some heterosexual people (that means men who love women and women who love men) dress in outrageous ways, but most don't.

It is important for kids to understand that gay love isn't sleazy, slutty, lusty love. It is simply love for the same sex. A gay person also has love for the opposite sex, not the marrying kind, but the father-son, mother-daughter, friend-to-friend stuff. *Gay* is simply a word for people who have different (different from the Anita Bryants) ideas of love.

### Finding Out That Your Parent Is Gay

The feeling a kid might have when he or she is told their parent is gay might be a very bad feeling. They might feel very resentful towards their parent who is gay and get angry or feel very confused about what it means. When they are told, they will probably be quite surprised and rather dumbfounded at first. But getting told something that you didn't expect is always a bit of a surprise.

Some kids might have a positive feeling. If he or she accepts the fact that their parent is gay then that's fine, and it's an easier thing to deal with. It's good for all kids to work toward feeling positive and comfortable with a homosexual parent.

### How Is Homosexuality Involved in Divorce?

Most kids never have to deal with their parent being gay. Many people believe that between 10 and 20 percent of all people are gay, which means that only one or two people out of ten will be gay. Many gay people never marry someone of the opposite sex, but some of them do because they don't realize that they're gay until they're older, or they don't accept it until then. A couple might decide to divorce because one of them is gay.

If the couple has children, the parent who isn't gay might feel that the influence of a gay parent is bad for a child and might make that child grow up to be gay. While we don't believe this is true, it can bring about legal problems involving custody rights.

The parent who isn't gay may take the other parent to court and try to keep them from having custody of the kids, or even visiting them.

A short time ago the court did not favor the gay parent, even if he or she was the "better" parent. They would take kids out of their mother's home if she was a lesbian. While times are changing, some kids are still forced to leave one of the parents against their will, just because that parent is gay.

Judge Edward Ginsburg of the Middlesex Probate & Family Court sometimes has to decide custody issues when one of the parents is gay. He told us that a case like this is no different than any other case. "The issue is what's in the best interest of the child. A parent's gayness is not a disqualification. It is a factor. If a mother puts her girlfriend—or boyfriend—before her child, it may not be best to give her custody." Judge Ginsburg has given custody to gay parents at times; other times he has not.

The judge also told us that this issue has changed a lot in the past few years. "Ten years ago," he said, "if a parent were gay he or she wouldn't have a chance to have custody. That's not true anymore. Now a judge or a jury must look at the facts and then decide."

## Living With a Gay Parent

Living with a gay parent is different from living with a parent who is not gay: instead of your parents going out with the other sex, they go out with the same sex. (Sure, your parents will go out with the other sex, too, but not in the same way, you know?)

If you live with a parent who is not gay and the parent you visit is gay, you might have trouble dealing with the situation. How do you deal with all the uncomfortable feelings (if you have any)? How do you feel when you visit your father or mother and they invite their boyfriend or girlfriend for dinner?

How about looking at it from a different angle—the "your-parent's-not-gay" angle. How do you feel when you visit your mother or father and they invite *their* boyfriend or girlfriend to dinner. It's not the same, you say? Why isn't it? If the person is the person your parent loves, why does it matter what sex they are?

If your parent is gay, how do you tell your friends? Do you tell them at all? Keeping it a secret might be harder than telling your friends because of "fag" and "dyke" jokes. If your best friend is really against gay people and he or she constantly ridicules them, maybe it would be better to inform him or her that your parent is gay and that they are no better or worse than anyone else because of it. That may be hard for you to do because of teasing and stuff like that. If you tell someone and they tease you, it's probably because they don't know what else to do, or they have never come into contact with someone who they knew was gay. Kids who don't know any lesbians or gay men are probably scared of the idea of being gay themselves or coming into contact with someone who is gay.

Use your own judgment about telling your friends; if you think they will be real jerks about it, don't tell them. If you feel like your friends will take it well, it might relieve some tension between you and them. You might feel it's none of your friend's business anyway. That's okay too; they're your parents and it's your life.

### Will This Affect Me?

Some kids ask themselves, "How will having a homosexual parent affect me?" A possible conclusion one might come to is that if your parent is gay, then you will take after your parent and also be gay. Some people think that having a gay parent will influence the child to be more affectionate toward people of the same sex, as their parent does, or to wear feminine or masculine clothes (depending on whether the gay parent is male or female).

Having a gay parent does not mean that a kid will be gay. If the kids *are* gay, then having a gay parent may make them feel much more comfortable with themselves and understand and respect their parent in a better way. Having a gay parent will enable the child to understand about different styles of life and different ways of having relationships with people.

We talked to some gay people and we saw some movies; we saw a television movie called "A Question of Love" about a lesbian mother's fight to keep custody of her kids. We also saw a documentary movie called "In the Best Interest of the Children" about lesbian mothers. Two books that can help kids to understand about being gay are *Growing Up Gay* by Youth Liberation Press and *Young, Gay and Proud* by a group of gay students and gay teachers from Australia.

Chapter **10**

# Do We Turn Out Differently?

## Myths

Before we started writing this book, we had a lot of discussions about the myths about divorce and about kids of divorced families. We got together as a large group, and we brainstormed the ideas of "experts" who supported the nuclear family and hated divorce. We wanted to think of all the bad things that people say might happen to the kids when their parents get a divorce. These myths say that kids of divorce

- would become mentally disturbed;
- would commit suicide at the age of 21 (80 percent of the time);
- would get rare diseases;
- would be on drugs;
- would become alcoholics;
- would become thieves and rob banks, steal cars, etc.;

- would get divorced themselves;
- murder their siblings;
- talk back to teachers;
- become violent;
- smoke pot in class;
- would be angry all of the time;
- would be lonely all of the time;
- have no friends;
- would think something's wrong with them.

We think these things are not true. Some people still think that a divorce will ruin a kid's life. While we disagree with this, we are aware that having divorced parents can change us in some important ways.

## Relating With Parents

A divorce will obviously have a great affect on you, your parents, and your relationship with your parents. You may feel that it was a "cop-out" for your parents to divorce, or you may feel a great disrespect for your parents after they divorce but realize that a divorce is probably one of the hardest things your parents will ever do and they have reasons for doing it. Divorce happens because two people feel that they can no longer live with each other. A good relationship with one or both of your parents before the divorce could make all the difference in the way you deal with them after the divorce.

Trust is a very hard subject to deal with. Trust is the issue you have to face when one of your parents goes out with someone new or if one of them remarries. It's feeling, "What if they break up again?" or "What if I have to go through a divorce again?" Will you still trust your parents to other relationships?

After a divorce, things may not be so good around your house. Your mom or dad might not "have it all together." Things around the house will probably get lost. So if you ask your parents for something and they don't get it for you, it's probably because they forgot, not because they don't love you. If your parent loses something that you asked them to hold on to for a while, it's probably because after a divorce, things can be very tough for your parents.

After a divorce a kid will usually live with one parent more than the other. Living with one parent *could* have its good points and its bad points. If there is more than one kid in the family and only one parent, it might be very hard to get any time alone with them (to talk with them), which would make it hard if you had any problems with your parent. You would have no one that's always there to talk to about problems you may be having with your parents, which might make it very hard to deal with those problems. Because of this, you might have to confront your parent with the situation. This could be very hard to do if you never have had to do it before, but in the long run, it could be very helpful to be able to talk with your parents more freely. Being able to deal with problems with your parents is very helpful in dealing with all the bad feelings of divorce.

After two people divorce, separate, or break up they may become paranoid and more cautious of the new people they go out with. (For some people, trying to start a new relationship just isn't worth the hardship they encounter when they break up.) They might become paranoid of all of the other sex. This could mean your parent might not want you out late at night, or they might tell you to be careful of who you go out with.

This might be a hard thing to deal with, but remember that your parent just lost someone who at one time was very close. (It could be very hard to be alone after having been married for a while.) If your parent feels paranoid or lonely, give him or her support, show him or her that the opposite sex is not all bad.

## Relationships with Friends

After a divorce, the way that we relate to our friends and our friends relate to us is an important matter. The fear of being treated like you have some rare disease after your parents' divorce is common. Even though these fears are not unreasonable, and it's not impossible for them to become reality, divorce is not a contagious disease.

Believe it or not, sometimes the person who is most afraid of these fears becoming reality, the kid of divorce, is the one who makes them happen. For instance, some kids whose parents are divorced think that talking to a friend about the divorce will make the friend shy off or think the kid is weird or strange. By not talking with a friend, you may just make the friend think, "Oh, he or she doesn't talk to me. He or she must be mad, or doesn't trust me." Sometimes when a kid whose parents are divorced feels like talking to a friend about the divorce, the kid's friend doesn't feel comfortable talking about such an important and frightening issue. Kids need a lot of support while their parents are going through a divorce. Friends help a lot.

Emily, a twenty-two-year-old woman whose parents were divorced when she was twelve, told us, "Being associated with other kids of divorce lessened the difficulty of the situation. If I didn't know anyone

Friendships will be more important to you.

whose parents were divorced, I would have felt really weird." Unless your friends think you are weird for having divorced parents, there's no reason to feel weird. Usually, even if a friend doesn't understand about divorce, he or she tries to help out.

Talking a lot about an important issue can bring people closer together (especially when the people have something to do with the issue). For instance, talking about divorce might bring people closer. Talking about the weather probably won't (unless one of the people is a weather freak). If two kids feel comfortable talking about the divorce, they'll probably both learn something about the other and maybe become closer. Many people believe that kids of one-parent families and/or divorce are more mature and choose older friends. Emily says, "Because my parents were going through terrible times, they didn't have time for the old me as the 'kid,' so that I had to become an adult much quicker in a sense."

Although Emily grew up quicker, she hung around with kids her own age. Some people say, "Yes, kids of divorce are more mature, but they pick friends of the same age."

## Are We More Grown Up?

We agree that children who have divorced parents tend to grow up faster than children whose parents are not divorced. They do not get taller or fatter or develop faster, but they tend to be more mature mentally. The reason for this is that children whose parents are divorced have more responsibilities because they have to take the place of the second parent who is not living at home, such as cooking dinner sometimes when their parent has to work late. Because the parents aren't living together anymore and are working during the day, there is no one at home to make the beds and clean the house. So kids have to be much more responsible and do many things that they probably didn't have to do when their parents were married.

Older children that have divorced parents often have to take care of the smaller kids. They have to babysit a lot and they have to play with the younger kids, too. The older brothers or sisters and the younger kids usually grow very close because they spend so much time together and usually go from one parent's house to the other house together.

All kids in divorced families have one thing in common: Their parents are divorced. This means that kids understand each other better than anyone else because they all have had the same experience. Of course, everyone's situation is not the same, but everyone has a little anger or sadness or some kind of feeling that is similar to someone else's.

Many kids whose parents are divorced think about some of their parents' problems. If there is a money problem in the house, a kid is much more aware of it because parents rely on the kids more often to help by sharing ideas. A parent also wants someone to talk to so that they don't feel alone. So kids that have divorced parents tend to have to think about adult problems to help support the family.

There are many different cases of responsibility. For instance, an only child has no brothers or sisters, so they have no one to support except their parents. However, they also have no one to support them. If the parent that the only child lives with works, the only child is alone a lot and has to do housework alone. This is very boring. So it is really nice if parents ask their kid to invite a friend over.

Chores are a very big part of a divorce. If your parents are divorced you will have many more chores because there is no one else to do them. You are only living with one person at the time, so you have to take the place of the other.

Living in two houses can be a reason why you would mature faster, because you have to travel a lot. If your parents live close together you don't have to go very far. If you are older you might use public transportation to go from one house to the other and learn about the city that way. If your parents live in different states, you are certainly going to learn something about airports or trains or some kind of transportation that you use to travel from one place to another.

You may also have two rooms that are yours, one at your mother's home and one at your father's. Having two rooms is really nice because you have much more room to store all of your things. Sometimes when you are at one house you want something that is at the other. That can be very inconvenient.

A boy in our class who we will call Greg had to take on a lot of responsibility when his parents got divorced. He had a little brother named George who was five years younger than he. Greg had to babysit all the time when his mother was working. He had to cook dinner, and he sort of became the father of the house. Greg had to support his younger brother when he was upset. His mother would discuss all her important problems with him so that he really took the place of the father.

Greg's situation can be good or bad. If you took the place of Greg you may think that he is really getting a lousy deal. On the other hand, Greg had a lot of responsibility and probably learned a lot about being a parent. Greg matured faster because he found out about real life. He learned how to cook and to take care of problems that are hard to take care of.

You can also be less grown up because of a divorce. A divorce is so upsetting sometimes that you do very badly in school. When you do badly in school, it can only upset you more. It is very hard to stay calm. The more you are under control, the more you can help your brothers, sisters, and parents through their pain.

Sometimes after a divorce, if you have two rooms and two households, you can get spoiled. If you are not used to having lots of space you may think it's great. Then maybe the parent that you don't live with most of the time buys you some presents or takes you somewhere special. If you get used to this luxury, you may come to expect it and get very spoiled. This, of course, doesn't happen to everyone.

After a divorce you could close up and become paranoid. You might not tell anyone that your parents are divorced. If you keep all your anger and sadness inside, it is much more painful. When you close up you can get very angry at people for very little things. You shouldn't let your anger out on people that you aren't angry at. It is a

good thing if you talk to a friend, because if you share your anger—
but don't get mad at them—they can help you.

Most kids who have divorced parents are slightly more grown up
than kids who don't have divorced parents. They have more responsibilities and they learn a lot from all their experiences. We wonder if
these benefits make up for the pain of the whole divorce?

## Well, Are We Different?

We asked a few kids of different ages, sexes, and different family
situations if they thought kids of divorce turn out differently than other
kids. "Well, in some ways they seem to be more mature," said a
thirteen-year-old boy whose parents are divorced. "Yes, I think they
(kids of divorce) grow up with more responsibility," said a thirteen-
year-old girl whose parents are divorced. A thirteen-year-old boy
whose parents are together agrees. "It's lonelier," says an eight-year-
old girl whose parents are divorced.

Whether in a negative or positive way, the kid of divorce will definitely be affected for the rest of his or her life. There are some positive
ways that one can be affected by a divorce: In choosing a mate or date,
the person, consciously or unconsciously, will remember their parents'
painful divorce and think more carefully about starting a relationship,
something that all people involved in relationships wish that they had
done. Another positive effect that divorce brings a person is simply the
whole family growing closer—not the mother and father, of course
—but the kids, and the separated parents to the kids. Negatively,
divorce can affect you in several ways. Kids who have seen divorce
sometimes think that all relationships end. Another side effect is the
pain. Sure, most of the pain is gone by the time a kid is an adult (or a
little younger), but some pain is still there. It will always be there.

And this is the final message of our book. We will not lie and tell
you that divorce has no effect on kids. It causes you to feel many things
and causes many changes in your life. You have to think of your family

and your world differently. But there will come a day when things will settle down, when you will be able to look back without the intense pain you felt earlier. While divorce never ends, it grows easier to live with until you learn to fully accept the fact that, for better or worse, you have lived through one of the hardest times any child has to experience. And all of us feel stronger when it's finally a part of our past.

# Books About Divorce

Our class read a whole lot of books, fiction and nonfiction, that had something to do with divorce. Some of the books were specially written to tell kids all about divorce. Some of the books were novels that had a character in the book whose parents were divorced. We read these books and talked about them. Some of us wrote reports. We also rated them to this scale:

☆☆☆☆☆ Excellent
☆☆☆☆ Good
☆☆☆ OK
☆☆ Neither Good Nor Bad
☆ Lousy

*How Does It Feel When Your Parents Get Divorced?* by Terry Berger (published by Julian Messner, 1977)

Sophie Gebhardt reviewed this book and rated it ☆☆☆☆☆.

A girl who is about twelve years old tells this story and it doesn't tell her name. The girl has blonde hair and is pretty small.

The girl's parents are getting divorced and we get to hear about the girl's feelings and how she coped with them. She tells how she was told about the divorce and her reactions. She first blamed herself. She wondered what would happen if her mother fell ill or died and whether her father would be able to take care of himself. The girl feels sad about the divorce. She also feels angry and tries to get back at her parents.

Sophie thought the best part was when the girl realized that she didn't have to choose between her parents and that she could love them both. Sophie liked the book a lot.

*Uncle Mike's Boy* by Jerome Brooks (published by Harper & Row, 1973)

Sophie Aikman reviewed this book and rated it ☆☆☆☆☆.

Pudge Lawents is twelve years old and his parents are going through a very difficult divorce. He is very close to his sister Sharon, and when she is killed by a truck he feels he has lost both his sister and his best friend. His parents can't deal with his feelings very well, so he seeks out his Uncle Mike, a man about 33, who enjoys seeing Pudge. Mike and Pudge become good friends.

This book seems pretty real because Pudge deals with his problems the way some of us dealt with ours.

*George* by E. J. Konigsburg (published by Atheneum, 1970)

Jon Tupta reviewed this book and rated it ☆☆☆☆.

Ben is a boy who adopts an imaginary character, named George, after his parents get divorced. He only acts out George in front of his brother Howard. "George" uses dirty words and does disgusting things and makes Ben's brother laugh. He also tries to be obnoxious, but his brother doesn't pay attention.

The boy doesn't deal with divorce very directly. It seems that the mother doesn't tell the two boys much about the divorce till it happens. The book shows one kid's way of dealing with divorce, which is putting all your true feelings into an imaginary character and then letting them out.

*My Dad Lives In A Downtown Hotel* by Peggy Mann (published by Doubleday, 1973)

Martin Albert reviewed this book and rated it ☆☆☆☆.

The book focuses on Joey, a boy of nine or ten and the only child in his family. He hears his parents fighting one night, then he hears the front door slam shut. In the morning Joey finds out that his father is not going to be living with him anymore. Joey thinks that it's his fault that his father left. Among the things he does is make a list of all his bad habits and promises his father that he won't do them again. Martin found this part sad.

At first Joey thought his father had just gone out to cool down after fighting with Joey's mom. When he found out that a divorce was going to happen, he felt alone, like his parents were the only ones to get divorced. He soon found out otherwise.

Parts of the story seemed realistic, like traveling in the city. One part of it seemed to be a contradiction. Joey seems to hate his father after he walks out. But then he makes a trip into the city all by himself to try to get this person he supposedly hates back. Martin didn't know if he would do a similar thing. It seems like Joey felt confusing feelings about his parents' divorce, but many kids feel confused.

*The Night Daddy* by Maria Gripe (published by Dell, 1971)

Beth Hammer reviewed this book and rated it ☆☆☆☆.

Julia is a girl who lives in a house with her mother. Her parents are divorced. Her mother works as a nurse on the night shift in a hospital. The Night Daddy is the babysitter who stays with Julia until her mother is home from the hospital.

Julia does not like that her parents are divorced and she is not happy that she has to have a Night Daddy. Later in the book Julia comes to face the divorce and makes friends with the Night Daddy.

*Talking About Divorce* by Earl Grollman (published by Beacon Press)

Hannah Gittleman reviewed this book and rated it ☆☆☆.

It is a book that is most useful for little kids and can be used by a parent or a big brother or sister to explain divorce to a little kid.

Each page contains two figures, like a child and a mother, and a sentence or two. It helps explain what happens in a divorce in a simple way.

The part Hannah liked best was the end, when they tell the best and the worst ways to tell kids about divorce.

*The Boys and Girls Book About Divorce* by Richard A. Gardner, M.D. (published by Bantam, 1971)

Louis Crosier reviewed this book and rated it ✫.

This is a nonfiction book that gives advice to kids whose parents are getting divorced. Louis liked the way the book was organized, but he didn't like much else. It is arranged in such a way that it first tells you things you should know about divorce in general and slowly it goes into other things, like who's to blame, love and anger, and how to get along with divorced parents and stepparents.

Louis felt that there are too many statements in the book that are abrupt and might not be suitable for younger kids. Parts of the book contained true statements, but they were written in a way that turned Louis off, with real talking-down to kids. While Louis did not like the book, many people do say that this is a great book on divorce and you might want to try it out for yourself.

## The Unit at Fayerweather Street School

The Unit at The Fayerweather Street School is a mixed-age group of 6th, 7th, and 8th Graders who learn and grow in an open classroom setting in Cambridge, Massachusetts. Fayerweather Street School has been a leader in the open education movement in this country and provides a safe, secure, and supportive environment in which children can emerge fully, explore, be challenged, take risks, and not fear making mistakes. The school respects and nurtures each child's individuality and helps children learn to respect their social and physical environment. Academic excellence, as well as physical and emotional growth, is nurtured in the context of rich and meaningful learning experiences.